MARK WILSON'S GREATEST
CLOSE-UP MAGIC TRICKS

More Than Forty Amazing Illusions
For Close Examination

An imprint of Running Press
Philadelphia • London

ACKNOWLEDGMENTS

The contents of this book do not represent the efforts of only two, three, or a dozen individuals; rather, they represent all those magicians of the past and the present who have labored so diligently to create, perfect, and present the Art of Magic.

Just as a stalagmite, buried unseen in a dark cave, builds from tiny drops into a towering structure, so has our Art increased through the centuries, shrouded in a like darkness of secrecy which remains a prerequisite to its growth.

With this book, you will join the ranks of those who have learned these inner secrets—and you must acknowledge and respect those whose contributions we enjoy. *Acknowledge* by being aware of the countless hours of study, work, and practice that have been expended by the magicians of the past to create our Art. *Respect* the magicians of today by never revealing any of these hard-earned secrets.

This, then, is the grateful acknowledgment of this book: *to the magicians of all times and places,* for their countless contributions to the Art of Magic.

Published and produced by arrangement with Ottenheimer Publishers, Inc. All rights reserved under the Pan-American and International Copyright Conventions. This book may not be reproduced in whole or in part, in any form or by any means, electronic or mechanical, including photocopying, recording, or by any information storage and retrieval system now known or hereafter invented, without written permission from the publisher.

9   8   7   6   5   4
Digit on the right indicates the number of this printing.

OPI MA024E

Printed in Hong Kong.

Library of Congress Cataloging-in-Publication Number 94-73874

ISBN 1-56138-569-7

Front cover photography by Weaver Lilley
Compiled by Caroline Schweiter
Edited by Liz Kaufman
Interior design by Ruthie Thompson

Published by Courage Books, an imprint of Running Press Book Publishers
125 South Twenty-second Street
Philadelphia, Pennsylvania 19103-4399

TABLE OF CONTENTS

ABOUT THE AUTHOR...
MARK WILSON

Mark Wilson has performed magic for more people than any other magician in the 3,500-year history of the art. During his successful career over the past 30 years, Mark Wilson has shared his wondrous magic with the world in many ways:

♦ Starred in the first weekly network magic series, *Magic Land of Allakazam*, which aired for two years on CBS, and for three years on ABC networks; six *Magic Circus* specials; *Magic of Mark Wilson* syndicated series; four *HBO Magic Specials*; *Magic of China, Children of China, Mr. Magic* syndicated specials; and many more.

♦ Developed international programming, including television specials for the NHK, NTV, and ASAHI Japanese networks and for Korea, Canada, Hong Kong, Australia, Great Britain, and People's Republic of China. Wilson's U.S. productions have aired throughout South America, Europe, Southeast Asia, Pacific Rim countries, and elsewhere.

♦ Authored *Mark Wilson's Complete Course in Magic*, the most popular book of magic instruction in history, with over 300,000 copies published.

♦ Served as creative consultant and supplier of magic to countless television series, such as *Columbo, Simon and Simon, Love Boat, Circus of the Stars, Perfect Strangers, Dear John,* and *The Odd Couple.*

♦ Instructs Hollywood's top stars in the performance of magic. Past and present celebrity students include Cary Grant, Tony Curtis, Peter Falk, Bill Bixby, Jackie Gleason, Cher, Johnny Carson, Burt Reynolds, and many others.

♦ Prepares entertainment packages for many of the world's finest theme parks, world's fairs, expositions, and major corporations worldwide.

♦ Most notably, in 1980 Mark Wilson was the first foreign magician to perform on mainland China since the founding of the People's Republic of China. He is the world's most honored magician, with *two* prestigious "Magician of the Year" awards and the "Master's Fellowship" from the Academy of Magical Arts. He has also won the "Superstar of Magic," "Magician of the Decade," and "Lifetime Achievement" awards.

INTRODUCTION

In magical parlance, Close-up Magic generally refers to tricks that are performed in an intimate setting, using small, everyday objects such as cards, coins, and balls.

Usually, Close-up Magic tricks are performed by a magician seated at a table with a small group of spectators, most often two to six people, seated alongside. However, the term can also be applied to performances for small groups of people, such as a gathering of family or friends in your living room. In such situations, the magician may stand while performing, so that all the spectators can see and enjoy the magic at the same time.

Therefore, Close-up Magic may encompass many different types of magic, suitable for performing in different situations. The tricks and routines in this book have been selected to give you a sample of a wide variety of magic.

As you read this book, you will see which tricks are better performed in a one-on-one setting and which tricks are best performed for groups. Because of the variety of the tricks you will learn, you will be able to increase your versatility and perform in practically any situation.

Some of the tricks require more practice and advanced preparation than others. Don't let practice scare you. One of the wonderful things about magic is that practicing and learning new tricks is half the fun!

Practice *is* crucial in magic, particularly when performing close to your spectators. Read the instructions carefully and study the illustrations. Rehearse in front of a mirror, so that you may catch yourself if you make a mistake.

And don't try to learn too much magic at once. Proceed slowly, one trick at a time, and move on. That way, you'll be sure to have a complete understanding of each and every trick before performing.

The tricks in this book may be some of the most powerful and effective magic you will ever learn. After all, if you can entertain and amaze spectators by doing magic right under their noses, you will join the ranks of the most revered and respected magicians in the world!

If you'd like to learn more about magic and take the next step in exploring our wonderful art, please write to me.

Happy Magic!

Mark Wilson
c/o Magic International
P.O. Box 801839
Santa Clarita, CA 91380-1839

CHAPTER 1

PREPARED
MAGIC

The ability to perform magic with ordinary objects is the mark of an expert magician. If you can work a miracle with a match, paper napkin, or water glass, then in the minds of the audience you must be a master prestidigitator.

After studying this chapter, you'll be able to cut two dollar bills in half and amazingly put them back together again! And you'll be able to borrow a dollar bill from a spectator and magically change it into an IOU. Upon your suggestion, the spectator will find the original borrowed bill inside a lemon! You'll also be able to tear a paper napkin into pieces and magically restore it to one piece. For a special twist, you will reveal the "secret" of the trick to the audience, giving them a logical explanation. But by the end of this explanation, your audience will be more baffled than ever before!

And now I'm going to let *you* in on the real secret to these tricks. Although they are all done with what appears to be ordinary objects, there is actually some secret preparation required. That's why we call this chapter Prepared Magic.

INFLATION

Here is a baffling cut-and-restore routine that is particularly effective when performed with real dollar bills. You can use play money, stage money, blank checks, or any form of printed paper about the size of regular currency.

EFFECT

You openly display two dollar bills and place them back-to-back. You then cut through the center of both bills with a pair of scissors, unmistakably cutting the two bills into four "halves." Without any suspicious moves, you instantly restore both bills to their original condition right before the eyes of the astonished spectators!

SECRET AND PREPARATION

A Place two new or crisp dollar bills face down on a table with the "green" side up.

B Apply a thin layer of rubber cement, about a ½" wide, down the center of the back (the green side) of each bill. When this is dry, add a second coat of cement and allow it to dry also.

C Next, sprinkle a little talcum powder on the cement-covered area on each bill. Spread the powder over the entire surface of the cement with your finger, or better yet, use a soft brush. You will notice that now the treated areas of

both bills will not stick to each other because of the powdered surface. Put the bills in your wallet or on your table, and you are ready to perform this very clever close-up mystery.

METHOD

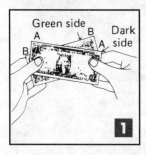
Green side / Dark side

1 Begin by removing the two pre-pared bills from your wallet and casually showing both sides of the bills. Place them back-to-back, as shown. (We will call the bill nearest you "Bill A," and the one nearest the spectators "Bill B.")

Both bills held together

2 Square up both bills. Be sure that the cemented areas are touching each other.

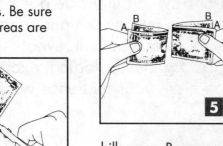

3 Hold both bills with the thumb and fingers of your left hand, as shown. With your right hand holding the scissors, carefully cut through the center of both bills. Make sure that you cut within the areas covered by the cement strips. Done

openly and deliberately, there will be no question in the spectators' minds that both bills have actually been cut in half—which they have.

4 Place the scissors aside. Grasp the halves on the right side of the cut in your right hand (half of Bill A and half of Bill B) and the halves on the left side (the other two halves of Bill A and Bill B) in your left hand.

5 With the thumb and fingers of both hands, separate the "halves" of the bills.

6 Shake the bills open. Because of the rubber cement, the halves in each hand will stick together at the cut edges, giving the illusion that the four "half" bills have "fused" together to form two complete bills!

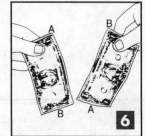

MARK WILSON'S GREATEST CLOSE-UP MAGIC TRICKS

COMMENTS AND SUGGESTIONS

Done well, this "quickie" is a real eye-popper. First, practice with stage money or with newspaper cut to the size of dollar bills. In this way, you will find out just how much rubber cement and talcum powder to apply. Then, if you wish, you can try it with real bills. These should be new and crisp and fit together neatly for Steps 2 and 3. Don't worry about losing money when using real bills, as the halves can be mended with transparent tape, just as with any torn bills.

MAGICIAN'S CHOICE FORCE

Maneuvering a spectator into selecting an object of your choice is called "forcing." Although the spectator believes there is a free choice, you are actually forcing him to choose the object you have prepared. The force you will learn here is called the MAGICIAN'S CHOICE FORCE. You can force the spectator to pick any of the three pieces of paper, but in this case you will force the piece of paper with the circle.

EFFECT

You will be able to correctly predict which of three drawings a spectator will select from the table.

SECRET AND PREPARATION

You will need three pieces of paper on your table. On one piece, you will have drawn a square; on the second, a circle; and on the third, a triangle. You will also need a spectator to assist you.

METHOD

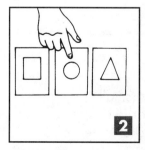

1 Point out to the spectator that you have drawn a different figure on each of three papers you have placed on the table. Ask the spectator to point to any one of the three slips. One of two situations will arise:

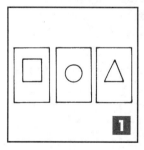

2 First situation: If the spectator points to the circle, say: "Would you pick up the paper that you have selected and hold it in your hand."

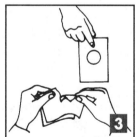

3 When the spectator does this, you pick up the other two papers and tear them up, saying: "We will not need these, so I'll tear them up."

4 Second situation: If the spectator points to the square or the triangle, you pick up the one they point to.

5 After picking up the spectator's choice, you say, "Fine, I'll tear this one up and that leaves only two."

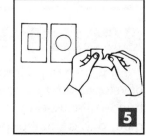

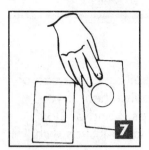

6 Ask the spectator to pick up either one of the remaining slips of paper. One of two things will now happen.

7 The spectator may pick up the paper with the circle on it.

8 If that happens, then you pick up the one remaining slip on the table and tear it up saying, "OK, the circle is the one you selected, so we won't need this one either."

9 The spectator may pick up the paper without the circle on it.

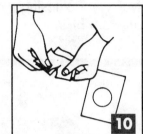

10 If that happens, you say, "OK, you tear up that slip, which leaves just the one on the table." Of course, the one that is left is the circle!

COMMENTS AND SUGGESTIONS

This is a very crucial trick for setting up other tricks. There is no sleight of hand or special skill needed. However, it is a trick that must be studied thoroughly and practiced until you can easily deal with each possible situation. After you have mastered it, you will be able to baffle your friends with one of the finest forces in the entire Art of Magic.

BILL IN A LEMON

BILL IN A LEMON is one of the great classics of modern magic. Several famous magicians have featured it as the highlight of their programs. There are several different versions of this mystery. In the clever method described here, no special skill is required. Thus it is an ideal trick for new students of magic as well as advanced practitioners.

EFFECT

From a bowl containing three lemons, a spectator is given a free choice of the lemons. The selected lemon is then placed in an ordinary paper or plastic bag, and the spectator holds the lemon throughout the entire presentation. After the lemon has been selected and is securely held by the spectator, you borrow a dollar bill and write its serial number on the back of a small envelope. You then insert the bill into the envelope, seal it, and give it to a second spectator to hold. You recap exactly what has happened up to this point. Then the spectator holding the envelope is told to tear it open and remove the borrowed bill. When this is done, the spectator finds, instead of the bill, an IOU for one dollar, signed by you. The first spectator is given a knife and asked to cut open the selected lemon, which has remained in that person's custody at all times. Inside the lemon, a tightly rolled dollar bill is found. When the bill is opened, its serial number is found to be exactly the same as the number written on the envelope, proving that the borrowed bill has magically traveled from the envelope to the inside of the freely selected lemon.

SECRET AND PREPARATION

For this amazing effect, you will need the following items: a stack of a dozen or more envelopes (small "pay" envelopes are best, but any small, opaque envelope can be used), three lemons, a bowl, a dollar bill, your handwritten IOU on a piece of paper that is the same size as a dollar bill, a rubber band, a pocket knife, some glue, and a small paper or plastic bag. A transparent bag is best.

HOW TO PREPARE THE ENVELOPES

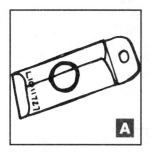

A To begin, write the serial number of your dollar bill on the back of one of the envelopes near the lower end, as shown. For future reference, this envelope has been marked with an "O" in the illustrations.

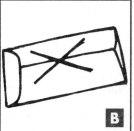

B Carefully cut off the gummed flap from another envelope. This envelope is identified with an "X" in the illustrations.

C This is how Envelopes X and O should look at this point.

D Fold the IOU and insert it into Envelope O.

I OWE YOU $1.00 YOUR SIGNATURE

E Place Envelope O on top of the stack of regular envelopes so that the written serial number is facing up, as shown.

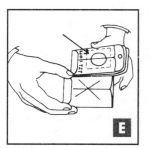

F Then place Envelope X (the one with the flap cut off) directly on top of Envelope O, concealing the serial number from view.

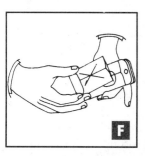

G Square up the envelopes and place the rubber band around the entire stack. Done properly, the gummed flap of Envelope O will appear to be the flap belonging to Envelope X.

HOW TO PREPARE THE SPECIAL LEMON

H Carefully remove the "pip" from one of the lemons with the point of a knife. Do not throw the pip away; you will need it later.

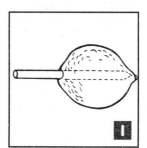

I Using a smooth, round stick (like the kind used for candied apples) or any similarly shaped slim, long object, carefully make a hole in the center of the lemon, as shown. This will expand the inner core area of the lemon and make the necessary space to accommodate a rolled bill. Be careful not to go too far and puncture the skin at the other end of the lemon with the stick.

NOTE: If a wooden stick of this type is not available, certain kinds of ballpoint pens and some pencils are thin enough to make the correct size of hole in the lemon. The important point here is that whatever object you are using be thin enough so that it does not puncture the inside, juicy portion of the lemon when it is inserted.

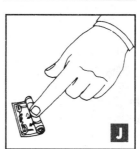

J Roll the dollar bill into a tight, compact cylinder.

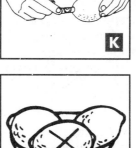

K Push the rolled bill completely into the lemon. Be sure that you have written down the serial number of the bill before you insert it into the lemon. Use a small dab of glue (model-airplane glue works well) to fix the pip back on the lemon. When you glue the pip back in place, adjust it so that it hides the small hole in the end of the lemon.

L Finally, place the prepared lemon (marked "X" in the illustration) in a bowl with two ordinary lemons. Be certain that you are able to distinguish the prepared lemon from the other two at a glance.

NOTE: There may be a special blemish on the prepared lemon that you can remember, or you can make a small mark with a black pen or pencil on the lemon that will not be noticed by the spectators.

M Place the bowl of lemons, the stack of envelopes, the pencil, the knife, and the small bag on your table. You are now ready to present this classic mystery.

METHOD

1 The "free choice" of the special lemon is accomplished by forcing, using the MAGICIAN'S CHOICE FORCE, which is described in detail on page 9. In this force, the spectator believes there is a free choice of any of the three lemons. Actually, you cleverly maneuver the spectator to select the special lemon. After the "selection" is made, pick up the small bag from your table. Hold the bag open and have the spectator drop the lemon inside. Tell the spectator to hold the bag tightly so that the lemon cannot get away!

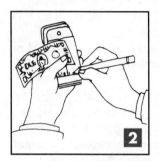

2 Borrow a dollar bill from one of the spectators. Explain that you will write its serial number on the top of the stack (Envelope X). As you pretend to copy the number from the borrowed bill, you actually write any number you wish on the envelope; it will automatically be switched for the correct serial number that is now hidden on the second envelope in the stack, Envelope O. (It is best if you remember the first letter of the serial number of your bill as this is the most obvious thing that the spectators might see and remember.) Just casually copy the number (with your first letter) of the borrowed bill. Remember, the spectators do not know what trick you are going to perform, so they will not pay particular attention to the serial number if you do not call attention to it.

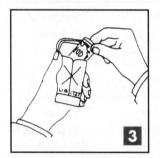

3 Fold the borrowed bill to about the same size as your IOU. Openly insert it into the flapless Envelope X. Be sure that everyone sees that the bill is definitely going into the top envelope of the stack. Be careful not to show that Envelope X does not have a flap.

NOTE: Inserting the bill into Envelope X requires some practice in the handling of the envelopes so that you can do it smoothly and not arouse suspicion. It may be helpful to remove the rubber band before attempting to insert the bill into the top envelope. This depends on how tightly the rubber band holds the packet of envelopes.

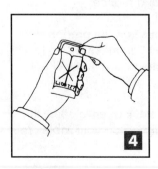

4 Once the bill has been inserted into Envelope X on the top of the stack, grip the uppermost flap (actually the flap of Envelope O) between your thumb and fingers and draw this envelope from the rest of the stack.

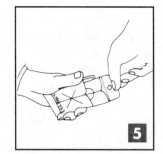

5 What you are really doing is drawing out Envelope O instead of Envelope X, but you hide that move from the spectators by turning the stack completely over as you draw the envelope clear.

6 This makes a perfect switch of Envelope X, the one containing the borrowed bill, for Envelope O, the one that contains your IOU.

7 Make sure Envelope O is entirely clear of the rest of the stack.

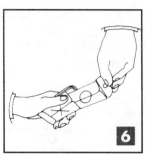

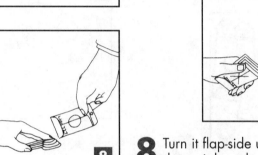

8 Turn it flap-side up so that the serial number that you previously wrote on Envelope O is clearly visible to the spectators. The spectators will be convinced that it is the same envelope and that everything is legitimate.

9 Immediately place the rest of the envelopes in your pocket, eliminating the possibility of anyone discovering that a switch was made. Seal Envelope O and give it to a spectator to hold.

10 Ask the spectator holding the sealed envelope to raise it toward the light to see that the bill is really there. Of course, what they actually see is the outline of your IOU.

11 Ask the first spectator to make sure the lemon is still in the bag. After the affirmative reply, ask the spectator if anything could have gotten inside the bag with the lemon. After the reply, recap what has happened up to this point. Explain that first you had one of three lemons selected and that the chosen lemon has been securely held by a spectator at all times.

12 Emphasize that you borrowed a dollar bill from a spectator after the selected lemon was safely in the bag held by another spectator. The serial number of the bill was recorded on the outside of an envelope, and the bill was sealed inside. Emphasize again that the envelope, with the bill still sealed inside, is now held by the second spectator.

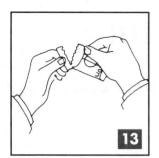

13 The trick is now already done, but the spectators don't know it! Ask the second spectator to tear open the envelope and remove the bill.

14 When the spectator opens the envelope, the IOU is discovered instead of the bill.

15 Give the knife to the person holding the bag with the lemon inside. Ask that spectator to remove the lemon from the bag. Once this is accomplished, take the bag from the spectator and hold it in your hand. With your other hand, give the spectator the knife and instruct that person to cut the lemon open. (It's even better if the spectator uses a pocket knife borrowed from another person!) Ask the spectator to rotate the lemon around the knife blade as if it had an inner core that should not be cut.

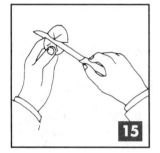

16 The spectator draws the halves of the lemon apart.

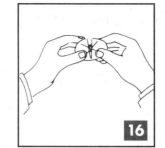

17 Inside, the spectator finds the bill imbedded in the center. Emphasize that you have never touched the lemon since it was selected from the bowl.

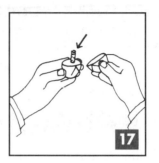

18 After the bill is removed from the lemon by the spectator, take the lemon halves and drop them into the bag. Put the bag on your table or casually toss it on the floor. (This subtly gets rid of the gimmicked half of the lemon so that it is not lying about where someone might pick it up and examine it later on.) Have the spectator compare the serial number on the bill that was in the lemon with that of the now

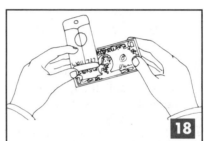

vanished, borrowed bill, which was written on the envelope. The spectator will find that the numbers are identical, proving that the borrowed bill has gone from the sealed envelope into the freely selected lemon—a magical miracle! Take back your IOU in exchange for the borrowed bill and thank the spectators for their assistance.

COMMENTS AND SUGGESTIONS

Be sure to write down the serial number of your bill before you load it into the lemon. Also, have the first letter of the serial number written somewhere handy for quick reference in case you forget it. You can strengthen the effect even more by writing the complete serial number of your loaded bill on Envelope X. To help you remember it, you may write the number very lightly (so that no one can notice it) on the back of Envelope X before the show. Another subterfuge for remembering the number is to have the number already written near the center of the envelope and then cover it with a wide rubber band. You can then shift or remove the rubber band toward you as you write. If you use this method, be sure to keep the stack of envelopes turned toward you as you write. When you have finished, you may display the stack freely to the spectators since the number matches identically the previously written number on Envelope O underneath. As for the rubber band, its main purpose is to keep the envelopes neatly in place during the early handling of the stack. Because it may prove helpful for the switch, the rubber band does not have to be removed from the stack during the performance unless it is too tight.

Another suggestion is to use an orange instead of a lemon. Because an orange is somewhat larger, it is easier to load, and you can easily withdraw the pip from the orange before inserting the bill.

It is a good plan to get several people to offer you a bill for the trick so you can pick the one that most closely resembles the age and wear of the bill already in the lemon. Also, don't give the owner time to note the serial number, since you are going to give back your bill instead of the one you borrowed.

As you can see, this is one of the truly great tricks in magic. You can build your reputation on this one trick alone, so study it and practice it before you perform it. Add your own touches. Emphasize the impossible nature of what the spectators have seen. Remember, always protect the truly marvelous secret of the BILL IN A LEMON.

TORN-AND-RESTORED DOLLAR BILL

EFFECT

You display a one-dollar bill front and back and then proceed to tear the bill into two parts. Not satisfied with just the halves, you put the two parts back together and tear through them both. You now have four separate pieces of a once-whole bill. You fold the torn pieces neatly into a small, square, green package and make a magical gesture over it. When you open the package, the audience is amazed to see that all of the pieces have mysteriously joined together to restore themselves into a completely undamaged bill.

SECRET AND PREPARATION

You will certainly want to practice this trick using stage money or play money. Or you may merely cut some pieces of paper to the correct "dollar bill" size for practice purposes. When performing for an audience, you may prefer to use real bills. This certainly strengthens the effect.

A Take one of the bills and place it flat on a table. "Accordion pleat" the bill into seven equal parts, as shown.

NOTE: On a "real" dollar bill, the face of the bill is printed in black while the back is printed in green. To make the rest of the steps clear, they will be described using a "real" bill.

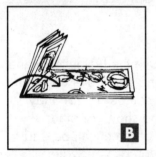

B With the bundle now folded into seven pleats, one of the outside surfaces of the packet will show part of the bill's face (dark side) while the other surface will show part of the bill's back (green side). Place the folded bill with the back (green side) next to the table. The face (dark side) is on top. Fold over one-third of the left side of the bill to the center, as shown.

C Fold over the other end (right side) of the bill, as shown. This last fold should bring the corner of the back (green side) of the bill to the top of the folded package. The complete folded package should appear as shown.

Glue here

D If the preceding three steps have been done correctly, you should have a small, flat package approximately ¾" square. Glue this packet to the back of a duplicate bill. Position the bills as shown. The glue is applied to the third of the bill that was next to the table when you folded the bill in Step C.

NOTE: If you use rubber cement, the bills can be easily separated after the show.

METHOD

1 Display the dollar bill to the audience, holding the bill opened out between the thumbs and fingers of both hands. Your left thumb serves two purposes: First, it keeps the duplicate folded bill from opening; second, it conceals the folded bill from being seen by any spectators located on the sides.

NOTE: You may wish to start the routine by holding the bill in your right hand with your right fingers on the side of the duplicate bill, completely hiding it from sight. This enables you to show the bill on both sides. Turn the face of the bill to the audience and transfer your grip on the duplicate bill from the fingers of the right hand to the thumb of the left hand.

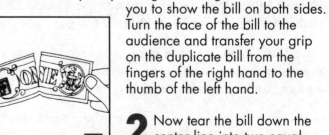

2 Now tear the bill down the center line into two equal parts, as shown.

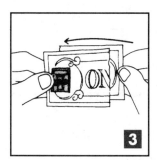

3 Place the right-hand half of the bill in front of the left-hand half.

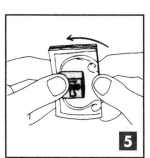

4 Grip the two halves between the thumb and fingers of both hands and tear both halves as shown.

5 Again, place the torn pieces in the right hand, in front of the pieces in the left hand, and square the packet. The torn pieces and the "secret" duplicate bill should appear to you as shown.

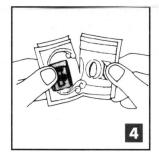

NOTE: A special touch can be added by first placing the torn pieces in the right hand to the rear of the packet held in the left hand. The four pieces can then be spread in a small fan and shown on both sides. The pieces at the rear will conceal the folded duplicate bill. Then, in squaring up the packet, you replace the rear pieces to the front and continue as follows.

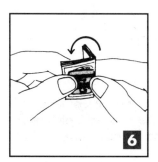

6 Fold the right-hand edges of the torn pieces forward so that they are even with the right side of the secret folded bill, as shown.

7 Fold the left-hand edges of the torn pieces forward, even with the left edge of the secret bill.

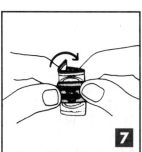

8 Fold down the top edges of the torn pieces even with the top edge of the secret bill.

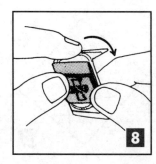

9 Do the same with the bottom edges, folding them upward and even with the bottom edge of the secret bill.

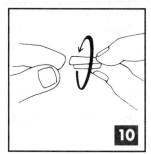

NOTE: You have now created a folded package of the torn pieces that matches exactly in size and shape the duplicate "whole" bill behind it.

10 Folded this way, the total package gives the impression of being only the folded pieces of the original bill. This makes it easy to casually turn the package over, showing both sides of the torn bill. When you finish showing both sides, be sure that you end with the duplicate "whole" bill in front and the folded torn pieces to the rear.

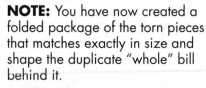

11 Make a magical gesture or say an appropriate magic word and begin unfolding the top and bottom thirds of the whole bill as shown.

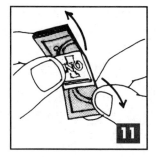

12 When these portions have been unfolded, grasp the right-hand edge of the pleated bill with your right thumb and first finger. Your left thumb holds the folded torn packet against the back of the bill, as shown.

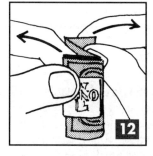

13 By pulling your hands apart, the duplicate bill unfolds so quickly it will appear to the spectators as if the torn pieces are instantly restored.

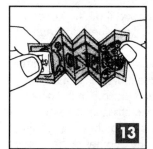

14 Briefly display the restored bill. Then fold it in half over the torn pieces, eliminating the possibility of accidentally exposing the torn packet as you return the "restored" bill to your pocket.

BROKEN-AND-RESTORED MATCH

EFFECT

You display a wooden kitchen match and give it to a spectator for examination. You spread out a pocket handkerchief on the table and place the match on the handkerchief near the center. You fold the four corners of the handkerchief over the match so it is hidden from view. You ask the spectator to grasp the match in both hands, through the folds of cloth, and break it into a number of pieces. Without any suspicious moves, you unfold the handkerchief, revealing the match completely unharmed and fully restored to its original condition!

SECRET AND PREPARATION

The secret to this mystery depends on the use of a certain type of handkerchief. It must be the kind that has a wide hem around the sides. This enables you to secretly conceal a duplicate match inside the hem. The spectators are never aware of the duplicate match.

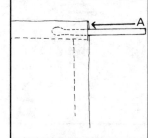

NOTE: Toothpicks may also be used quite effectively in this trick instead of matches.

To prepare, carefully insert the match into the open end of the hem of the handkerchief. Push it just far enough inside so that it is completely hidden from view. In the illustrations, the corners of the handkerchief have been labeled A, B, C, and D, with the match inside the hem at Corner A. Fold the handkerchief and place it in your pocket and have a box of duplicate matches handy for the presentation.

METHOD

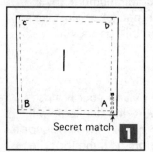

Secret match

1 Display the box of matches and open it, requesting that a spectator select one match to use in the trick. Remove your handkerchief (with the secret match hidden in the hem) and spread it on the table in front of you. Place the handkerchief so that the hidden match is in the lower right-hand corner (A), nearest you. Take the match from the spectator and place it in the center of the handkerchief, as shown. Note that both matches are running parallel to one another at the start.

2 Fold Corner A up and over the center of the handkerchief, placing the secret match by the selected match. Notice that the selected match and the secret match are now perpendicular to each other. This way, it will be easy for you to distinguish which match is which, without having to see them. You can rely upon your sense of touch to tell them apart.

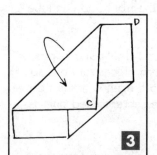

3 Fold the top left Corner C over the selected match and over Corner A, as shown.

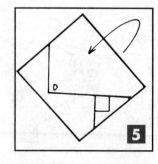

4 Fold Corner B over Corners A and C as in the illustration.

5 Finally, bring Corner D over Corners A, B, and C, as shown.

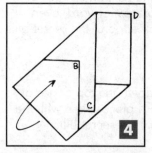

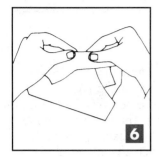

6 Openly and deliberately grasp the secret match through the folds of the handkerchief and hold it between the thumb and fingers of both hands. You can be sure to grasp the secret match easily by simply "feeling" for the match that runs parallel to the edge of the table nearest you.

NOTE: The selected match remains within the handkerchief.

7 Hand the secret match to the spectator.

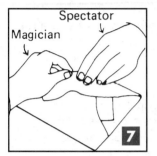

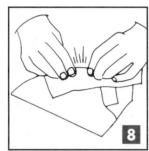

8 Instruct the spectator to break it several times through the fabric of the handkerchief. The spectator believes the match that

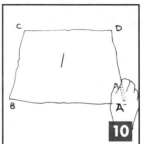

was just selected and that you folded inside the handkerchief is the one being broken.

9 When the spectator is quite satisfied that the match has been completely destroyed, slowly and deliberately unfold each corner of the handkerchief, one at a time.

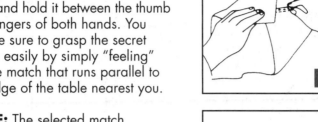

10 As you unfold Corner C with your left hand, keep your right hand over Corner A to conceal any possible bulge of the hem that might be caused by the pieces of the secret match. When you have completely opened the handkerchief, the spectators will be amazed to see that the broken match is now fully restored.

11 Immediately give the match to the spectator for examination. Hold up the handkerchief, shake it, and show it on both sides so that all can see that it is completely empty before you casually replace it in your pocket.

BAG-TAG ESCAPE

EFFECT

You display what appears to be a typical baggage tag and give it to the nearest spectator to examine. A second spectator is given a length of string to examine. The tag and the string prove to be normal in every respect. You proceed to thread the string through the small hole in the tag. You give one end of the string to each spectator to hold. With the tag hanging in the center of the string, you cover the string and the tag with a pocket handkerchief. Reaching beneath the handkerchief, you "magically" remove the tag from the center of the string without damage to either! The spectators are left holding the now empty string suspended between them with no explanation for the mystery they have just witnessed.

SECRET AND PREPARATION

For this trick you will need to construct some small tags from cardboard. Filing-card stock is best. The tags should be cut so that they measure approximately 3" x 1½" in size. Shape the tags by cutting off the two top corners at a 45° angle and punch a hole in the center of the top edge of each of the tags, as shown. The result will be a tag that closely resembles a standard baggage tag in every respect except one. Most standard tags are heavily reinforced around the small hole so that they will not tear when fastened to some object. This slight difference is what makes the entire effect possible. You will also need a piece of string about 2' long, which you place on the table along with one of the tags. Place an ordinary handkerchief in your left pocket and a duplicate tag in your right coat sleeve so that it is out of view of the spectators.

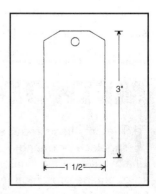

METHOD

1 To begin the presentation, ask for the assistance of two spectators. Hand one of the spectators the tag for examination and the other spectator the length of string. When they are satisfied that everything is unprepared, thread the string through the small hole at the top of the tag, as shown in the illustration.

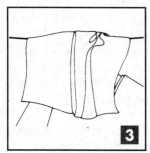

2 Give one end of the string to each spectator, leaving the suspended tag imprisoned on the string.

3 Remove your handkerchief from your pocket, show it to be completely empty, and cover the tag and the center of the string, as shown. Be sure the handkerchief is spread open enough to provide the cover necessary to conceal your hands beneath it. Reach under the handkerchief with both hands and grasp the tag near the hole at the top.

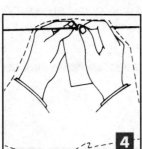

4 Carefully and quietly tear through the tag to the hole. Remove the torn tag from the string.

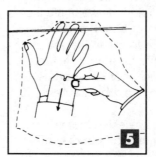

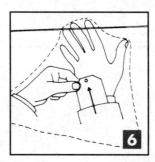

NOTE: You may find it helpful to raise both hands slightly upward, thus lifting the handkerchief away from the tag. This will prevent the spectators from seeing the motion of what is actually taking place.

5 With the fingers of your right hand, secretly insert the torn tag into your left coat sleeve.

6 Exchange hand positions so that your left hand can withdraw the duplicate tag from your right sleeve, as shown.

7 Now for the startling climax. Bring both hands into view along with the duplicate tag. Ask the spectators to look beneath the handkerchief to see if you actually removed the tag from the string, as it appears. You may then offer the tag, the string, and the handkerchief for examination.

LIFESAVERS® ON THE LOOSE

EFFECT

You display an ordinary shoelace and hand it to a spectator for examination. Reaching into your pocket, you remove a new package of Lifesavers candy and give it to another spectator to open. A number of the Lifesavers are then threaded onto the shoelace, and the ends of the lace are handed to two spectators to hold. Removing the handkerchief from your pocket, you cover the Lifesavers dangling in the middle of the lace, concealing them from view. Reaching under the handkerchief, you magically remove the imprisoned Lifesavers, leaving the now empty shoelace suspended between the two spectators.

METHOD

1 The only items required for this effect are an ordinary shoelace or a length of string, and a package of Lifesavers or some similar candy with a hole in the center. To begin the presentation, hand the shoelace to a spectator for examination while you introduce the package of Lifesavers to another spectator to open.

2 Pick up one of the Lifesavers and thread it on the shoelace, as shown.

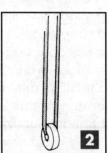

MARK WILSON'S GREATEST CLOSE-UP MAGIC TRICKS

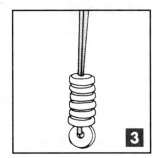

3 With the candy suspended from the center of the lace, thread the remaining Lifesavers on the shoelace by running both ends of the lace through the holes in the candy, as shown.

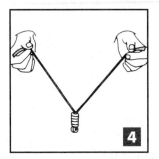

4 Give both ends of the shoelace to a spectator to hold; or give one end of the lace to one spectator and the other end to another spectator to hold. Either way, have the spectator(s) hold the ends far apart to allow enough space to drape your handkerchief over the suspended Lifesavers.

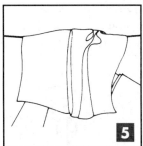

5 Remove your handkerchief and cover the Lifesavers, as shown. Be sure to spread open the handkerchief along the shoelace to provide enough cover for your hands when you place them underneath.

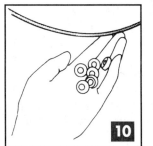

6 Reach under the handkerchief with both hands.

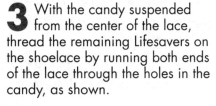

7 As soon as your hands are out of view, grasp the bottom Lifesaver between both hands and break it in half, as shown.

8 Try not to break it into little pieces, as these can be difficult to conceal in your hand and may also fall to the floor during

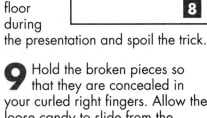

the presentation and spoil the trick.

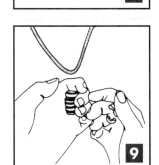

9 Hold the broken pieces so that they are concealed in your curled right fingers. Allow the loose candy to slide from the shoelace into your left hand.

10 With your right hand still concealing the broken pieces, lift the handkerchief away from the shoelace, revealing the loose Lifesavers in your left hand.

11 Place the handkerchief back in your pocket along with the broken pieces, and the mystery is complete.

® Lifesavers is a registered trademark of Lifesavers, Inc.

COMMENTS AND SUGGESTIONS

This is truly an ideal impromptu mystery. All of the items are ordinary and easily obtainable. Just be sure to thread enough Lifesavers on the string, and no one will miss the broken one—the real secret of this clever mystery.

 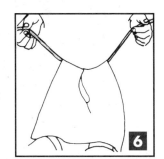

CORDS OF FANTASIA

EFFECT

You borrow two finger rings from spectators. Handing one of the spectators a pencil, you display two shoelaces. These laces are secretly tied around the pencil. Both rings are threaded onto the shoelaces and held in place with an overhand knot. Under these conditions, even with the spectator holding onto the ends of the laces, you cause the rings to magically "melt" through the cords, leaving the rings, pencil, and laces intact!

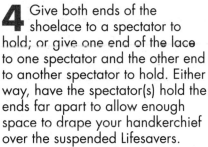 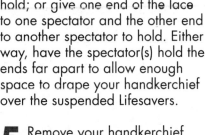

SECRET AND PREPARATION

All you will need are a pencil, a pair of shoelaces, and the two finger rings. All of the props are quite unprepared, and this clever effect can be presented at any time and any place that these common items can be obtained.

METHOD

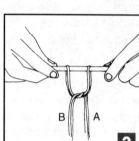

1 Begin by borrowing two finger rings from spectators. Have one spectator hold the pencil by the ends. Drape the two shoelaces over the pencil, as illustrated. From this point on, we will refer to these as Lace A and Lace B.

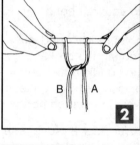

2 While the spectator holds the pencil, grasp both strands of Lace A in your left hand and both strands of Lace B in your right. Tie a single overhand knot, as shown.

3 Pull the knot up tight and ask the spectator to release the grip on the pencil. Turn the laces so that they are now parallel to the floor and the pencil is held by the laces in an upright position. Pull the laces tight on the pencil so that the pencil does not slide out. Hand the ends of the laces to the spectator.

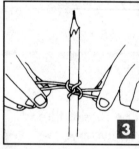

4 Call attention to the two borrowed finger rings and thread them onto the laces. Thread one ring on each side of the pencil, as shown. Be sure to put both strands of Lace A through one ring and both strands of Lace B through the other.

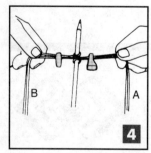

5 You are ready to tie the rings in place. To do this, take one of the B ends and one of the A ends. Tie those ends in a single overhand knot, as shown. You will notice that when you tie this knot, you are crossing an A end with a B end. It makes

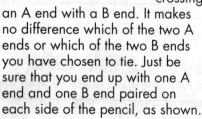

no difference which of the two A ends or which of the two B ends you have chosen to tie. Just be sure that you end up with one A end and one B end paired on each side of the pencil, as shown.

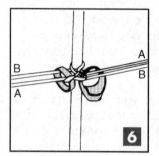

6 Pull this new knot up tight. The rings will be jammed against the pencil. Hand the ends back to the spectator so that the spectator is now holding the entire affair, as shown.

7 With your right hand, grasp the knot on the pencil, as shown. With your left hand, hold the pencil near the bottom and prepare to slip it free of the knot.

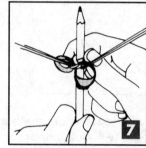

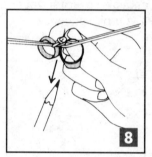

8 With your right hand firmly holding on to the knot, pull the pencil out of the laces with your left hand.

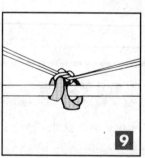

9 Thread the pencil through the rings. Note that the right hand, which still holds the knot firmly, has been eliminated from this illustration for clarity.

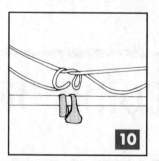

10 Ask the spectator to pull on the ends of the laces. At the same time, release your grip on the knot held by your right hand. The illusion is perfect. The rings seem to melt right through the laces!

11 The spectator is left holding only the two laces; the rings are on the pencil. Immediately allow the spectators to examine everything and return the rings to their owners with your thanks.

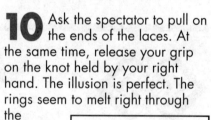

EAST INDIA ROPE TRICK

In the real East India Rope Trick, a large rope rises mysteriously in the air and then a small child climbs the rope. For your presentation, you make a cardboard tube mysteriously rise up and down with two strings.

SECRET AND PREPARATION

To present this trick, you will need an 8½" x 11" piece of cardboard, two 3' strings, cellophane tape, and a paper clip.

A Roll the cardboard to make a tube and fasten the sides of the cardboard together with cellophane tape, as shown.

B Fasten the middle of String A to the bottom of the tube with a paper clip. Then thread String B through the middle of String A. Bring String B out through the top of the tube and String A out through the bottom of the tube. Study the illustration to see how the strings are "hooked up" inside the tube.

METHOD

1 To present the trick, hold the tube vertically before the audience with String A in your bottom hand and String B in your top hand, as shown.

2 Keeping the strings taut, make the tube "float" up by pulling String A down. Then, make the tube "float" down by allowing String A to slide up. Repeat several times.

COMMENTS AND SUGGESTIONS

When you have finished the trick, secretly remove the paper clip and Strings A and B, and let the audience examine the tube.

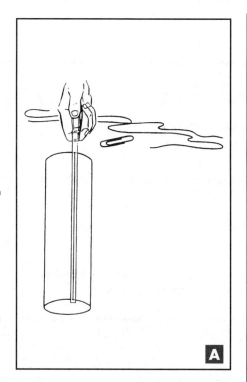

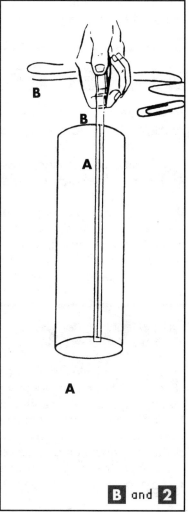

CLIPPO

EFFECT

This clever cut-and-restore effect works on the same principle as INFLATION, described on page 8. You display a single column cut from the classified section of a newspaper. Folding the paper strip in half, you cut away the folded center, leaving two separate strips of paper. When you "unfold" the two individual strips, you find that the news column has mysteriously restored itself back to one piece! It seems as though the ends of the strips have magically "healed" together. Somewhat puzzled at this strange occurrence, you repeat the cutting process, this time cutting the center fold at an angle. To everyone's surprise, when the paper is unfolded it is again found restored— with a sharp bend in the center of the column! Finally, the paper strip is cut for the last time, and is once again restored to its original form.

SECRET AND PREPARATION

To prepare for this trick, you will need the classified section from a newspaper, scissors, rubber cement, talcum powder, and a tissue.

A With a pair of sharp scissors, cut a single ad column from the classified section of a newspaper. The column should be about 24" long.

B Place the strip of paper on the table and apply a thin coat of rubber cement all along the center section of one side as shown and allow it to dry. Next, sprinkle a little talcum powder on the treated (rubber cement) area. Spread the powder over the entire surface with a tissue or soft brush. (The powder will prevent the treated surfaces from sticking together when the strip is folded in half.) This done, you are now ready to present this clever mystery.

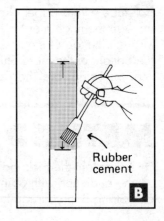

Rubber cement

B

METHOD

1 Begin by displaying the paper strip and making some comment about the large variety of items that you can find advertised in the newspaper. This is a good opportunity to inject comedy into the routine by pretending to read some humorous ads. These are really ads that you have memorized and should be as crazy and absurd as you can make them. As an example: "For Sale: Used tombstone—great buy for someone named Murphy!"

2

2 After apparently reading the first ad from the center of the column, fold the news strip in half so the treated surfaces of the paper are together.

3 Using the scissors, snip off the fold in the center of the strip, making sure to cut straight across the paper. Make this cut in the pretense of cutting away the advertisement which you just read.

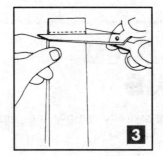

3

The section cut away should be no more than ½" wide. Make sure that the cemented areas are touching each other before making the cut. Done openly and deliberately, there will be no question in the audience's mind that the strip has actually been cut into two pieces . . . which it has.

Secret joint →

4

4 Now carefully open out the paper strip, revealing it restored into one piece! Because of the rubber cement, the paper strips will stick together at the cut edges, giving the illusion that the news column has restored itself. Even at a slight distance, no one will notice that the strip is secretly "joined" at the center.

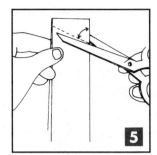

5 Pretend to read another crazy ad and then fold the strip again and snip off another section from the center. This time, instead of cutting straight across, cut the paper at an angle to the right as shown.

6 When you open the paper strip, the rubber cement will again restore the two pieces, but the upper half of the paper will veer off to the right at a sharp angle!

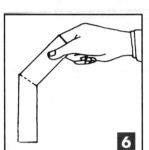

7 Repeat the cutting process again. This time cut the strip at an angle to the left.

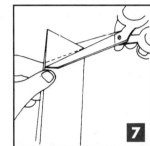

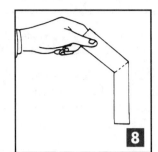

8 When the paper is opened, the upper half will veer off to the left, as shown.

9 Finally, fold the paper in half again and cut it for the last time—straight across—as in Step 3.

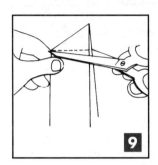

10 When opened, the paper strip will appear to be restored to its original condition in a straight column.

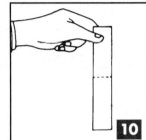

11 To conclude, fold or crumple the piece of newspaper and place it aside, out of reach of the spectators.

COMMENTS AND SUGGESTIONS

Play up the cutting of the paper for laughs by appearing to be confused every time a section is cut away. Each time you make a "mistake," try to solve the problem by cutting a little more of the paper away. An audience is always amused when they think that you have made a mistake, so ham it up a bit and your audience will enjoy the trick even more.

SUCKER TORN-AND-RESTORED NAPKIN

EFFECT

Displaying two napkins, you announce that you are going to "teach" the spectators how to perform a trick. One napkin you crumple into a ball and show how you secretly palm it in your left hand. You explain that this is a "secret" napkin, which none of the spectators is supposed to know about. You tear the other napkin into a number of pieces. Now for the secret. You demonstrate exactly how you cleverly switch the torn napkin for the secret napkin. You even open up the secret napkin to show how the torn pieces have supposedly been restored. The spectators, believing that they know how the trick is done, are warned by you that, if they should ever perform the trick, never to let anyone see the torn pieces in their hand. You explain that if that should ever happen, they would need to restore those pieces by magic. With that, you open the torn pieces, revealing that they too have been restored into a whole napkin! It is then that the spectators realize that they have been taken in by you all along.

SECRET AND PREPARATION

A To perform this highly entertaining effect, you will need three identical paper napkins. In this illusion, the napkins are numbered 1, 2, and 3. To prepare, spread open two of the napkins (1 and 2) and place one napkin (2) on top of the other napkin (1). Crumple the third napkin (3) into a

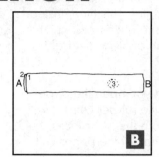

ball and place it at the bottom center edge of the open napkins, as shown.

B Starting at the top edge, roll the two open napkins down into a "tube" around the third napkin.

METHOD

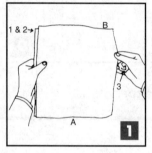

1 To begin, pick up the tube in your right hand near the center. Hold the tube so that End B is on top. Hold the third napkin (3) through the other two napkins (1 and 2). With your left hand, grasp the edges of the tube and start to unroll the open napkins (1 and 2) with your right hand. You should be able to feel the third napkin (3) inside as you unroll the tube. When the napkins are completely opened, secretly roll the inner crumpled napkin (3) into your right fingers, as shown, so that it is hidden from the spectators.

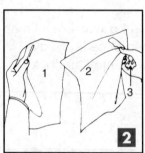

2 Separate the two open napkins, taking one napkin (1) in your left hand and the other napkin (2) in your right. Announce to the spectators that you are going to teach them how to perform a trick.

3 Explain that one of the two napkins (1) is a secret napkin and must be concealed in your left hand until the proper moment. As you say this, with your left hand crumple the left-hand napkin (1) into a ball. Hold it in the curled fingers of your left hand, the same as the third napkin (3) in your right hand (of which the spectators are totally unaware). Explain to the spectators that this secret napkin must be secretly palmed in your left hand at all times as you perform the trick.

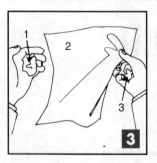

4 Explain that the trick begins when you tear the whole napkin (2) into a number of pieces, which you proceed to do. Roll these torn pieces into a small ball.

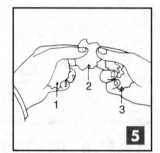

5 Here's how your hands should look from your point of view. The napkin (2), between the tips of your thumbs and fingers, is the torn one; the napkin (1) in your left hand is the secret napkin that the spectators know about; and the napkin (3) in your right hand is the one only you know about.

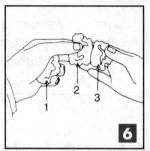

6 As you are finishing, roll the torn pieces (2) into a ball and secretly add to them the whole napkin (3) in your right hand.

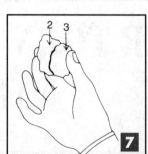

7 Show both napkins (2 and 3) together as if they were just the torn pieces. As you display the supposedly torn pieces—really the torn pieces (2) and the third whole napkin (3)—turn your right hand so the spectators can see that it is quite empty. This is a very important part of the trick. It convinces the spectators that everything is on the level, so that they will not suspect there is a third napkin.

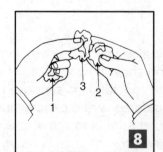

8 Pretend to roll these pieces (Napkins 2 and 3) into a smaller ball. As you do, secretly draw the torn pieces (2) downward, behind your right fingers with your right thumb. This leaves only the whole napkin (3) at the tips of your right fingers.

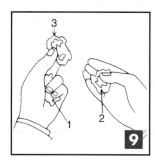

9 Transfer only the whole ball (3) to the tips of your left fingers, as if it were the torn pieces.

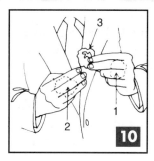

10 The spectators think that you have merely placed the torn pieces, which they just saw you crumple into a ball, into your left fingers. Here is the spectators' view of this action.

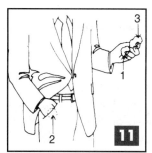

11 Explain that when they (the spectators) perform this trick for their friends, they should have a coin in their right pocket to use as a sort of magic wand. With your right hand, reach into your right pocket and bring out the coin. When you do, leave the torn pieces (2) in your pocket.

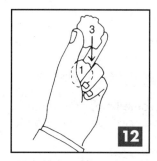

NOTE: The spectators will not suspect anything because you have offered a logical reason for placing your hand in your pocket. This is a very important lesson to be learned by all magicians: There must be a reason for every move you make. Otherwise you will arouse suspicion and, more than likely, spoil the entire effect.

12 At this point, the spectators still believe that the torn pieces are held at the tops of your left fingers and the secret whole napkin is hidden in the curled fingers of the same hand. Actually, both of these napkins (1 and 3) are whole.

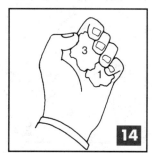

13 Tell the spectators that the real reason for getting the coin is to direct attention away from your left hand so you can execute the switch. Explain that when your right hand reaches into your pocket, the spectators' eyes follow it, leaving your left hand free to do the dirty work.

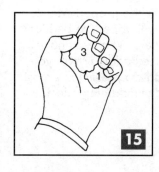

14 Openly demonstrate this dirty work (the switch). Slowly draw your left thumb and fingers down into your left hand.

15 Bring the supposedly torn pieces (3) along.

16 Move your thumb over to the secret napkin (1).

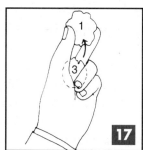

17 With the aid of your third and little fingers, raise this napkin (1) up to the tips of the fingers. Execute this series of moves slowly and deliberately with the palm of your left hand toward the spectators, to show them exactly how the switch is made.

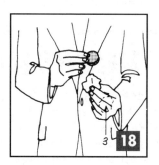

18 Explain that at exactly the same time the switch is being made in the left hand, you remove the coin from your pocket with your right hand. Wave the coin over the napkin(s) and replace it in your pocket.

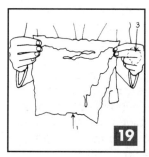

19 State that all that remains is to open the secret napkin and show it restored, and do just that.

20 Caution the spectators that they must always be very careful not to accidentally show the torn pieces concealed in their hands as they unfold the napkin, "as that would be very embarrassing." There is one thing, however, they can do to save themselves if that should ever happen.

21 The only thing you can do in that case is to restore the torn pieces. As you say this, open up the napkin (3), which the spectators believe to be the torn pieces, and show it to be completely restored! It is then that the spectators will realize you have baffled them once again!

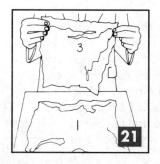

22 Pick up both napkins (1 and 3) and hold one in each hand. Show both of your hands to be unmistakably empty as you toss the completely restored napkins to the spectators.

DOTS MAGIC

After you become known as a magician, you will often be asked to perform while you are seated at a table. The following effect teaches you a sleight, the Paddle Move, that is ideal under these very conditions.

EFFECT

You display a clean table knife. After polishing both sides of the blade with your napkin, you attach three red dots, one at a time, to the top surface of the blade. As you attach each dot, three identical dots appear on the opposite side of the knife, one at a time, as if in sympathy with the first three dots. You hand the knife to a spectator seated near you and ask that the person verify the existence of the duplicate set of dots. Upon retrieving the knife, you remove the top three dots from the blade and, magically, the bottom three dots vanish in sympathy. Suddenly all six dots reappear, three on each side of the knife blade. You remove the dots, one at a time, from the top of the blade. As you remove each dot, the corresponding dot on the bottom vanishes in perfect synchronization. With the table knife as clean as it was in the beginning, it is again handed to a spectator for examination.

SECRET AND PREPARATION

A The small, circular dots needed for this effect are available at your local stationery store. They are self-adhering and come in several colors. Red has a high visibility and is therefore recommended for the trick, but any color will do. (If you wish, you can even cut dots out of gummed paper, but the pressure-sensitive commercial dots can be much more easily attached and removed for this particular routine.) The dots selected should measure about ¼" in diameter.

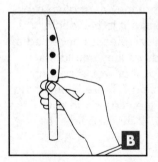

B For practice purposes, prepare the table knife by placing three of the dots on one side of the blade, as shown. Turn the blade over so that the blank side is face up.

C The next step is the classic turn, entitled the Paddle Move. After you have learned it, you will be able to show the blank side of the blade twice as you turn the knife over in your hand, apparently showing both sides. This will leave the spectators with the impression that they actually saw both sides of the blade. This is the one sleight used in this entire routine. It is one of the most valuable principles in close-up magic.

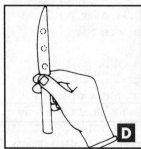

D To perform the Paddle Move, pick up the knife between the thumb and first two fingers of your right hand by the handle, as shown. The blank side of the blade should be facing up. You will notice that the blade is facing away from you (pointing toward

the spectators). It should be held at about waist level. You are about to turn the knife over so that the blade points toward you. To prevent the dots fastened on the bottom of the blade from being exposed, you must simultaneously revolve the knife between your thumb and first two fingers as you turn the knife over.

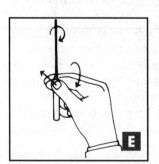

E Your right thumb rolls the knife handle with your thumb and fingers one half-turn to your left.

F At the same time, you rotate the blade over so that it points toward you.

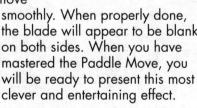

G Rotate the blade back toward the spectators. At the same time, execute Steps E and F in reverse and roll the knife back (to your right) with your thumb and fingers so that the blank side is still up. Practice in front of a mirror until you can execute the move

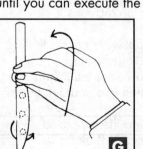

smoothly. When properly done, the blade will appear to be blank on both sides. When you have mastered the Paddle Move, you will be ready to present this most clever and entertaining effect.

H Before the performance, place six of the dots in your wallet (or an envelope). After you are seated at the dinner table and have the opportunity, secretly attach three of the dots to the underside of the blade of your knife. You are now ready to perform a minor miracle.

NOTE: The illustrations depicting the Paddle Move above, as well as those in the Method that follows, are from the magician's point of view, as the knife is held horizontally over the surface of the table.

METHOD

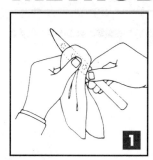

1 Stand up and display the knife to the spectators. Using the Paddle Move, show both sides of the blade to be empty. (Really, there are three dots on one side.) Wipe both sides of the blade, one side at a time (really the same side twice, using the Paddle Move), with your napkin to further create the illusion of a clean knife.

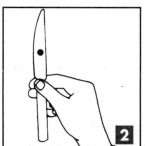

2 Remove the three remaining dots from your pocket and set them on the table. Place one of these directly in the center of the blank side of the blade, as shown.

3 Display the dot and execute the Paddle Move to apparently show the opposite side of the blade. To the spectators, it will appear that a duplicate dot has magically appeared on the other side of the blade.

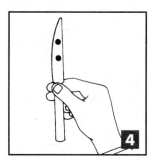

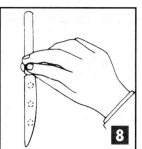

4 Return the knife to its original position and attach the second dot near the end of the blade, as shown.

5 Execute the Paddle Move again and apparently show the arrival of the second dot on the back of the blade.

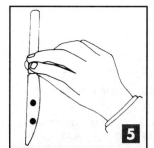

6 Repeat Step 3 with the third and last dot, again showing the knife on both sides. The spectators will now be convinced that the blade of your knife has three dots on both sides. At this point, it

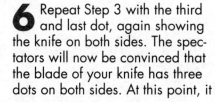

actually does have three dots on both sides because of the three, secret dots you previously attached. Hand the knife to a spectator for examination.

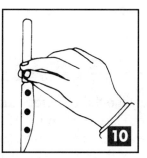

7 As soon as the knife is returned to you, openly remove the three dots from the top of the blade and put them in your pocket.

8 Execute the Paddle Move and show that the three dots on the back of the blade have vanished as well.

9 Pick up your napkin and apparently wipe the blade clean. Under cover of this wiping action, turn the blade over. The spectators will be surprised to see that the three dots have reappeared on the knife!

10 By executing the Paddle Move, you can show that the dots have magically returned, not only to the top of the blade but to the back as well.

NOTE: At this point you are set up for the vanish of the dots, one at a time, since the blade now has three red dots on the top surface only. Simply repeat Steps 2 through 6 in reverse.

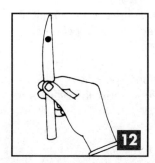

11 Begin by removing the center dot and executing the Paddle Move. It will appear as if the center dot vanished from the back of the knife as well.

12 Remove the dot closest to the handle and apparently show both sides, as before. This will leave you with one dot on the tip of both sides of the blade.

13 Remove the last dot and slowly show both sides of the knife. The blade will be clean of spots and may now be handed to the spectator for examination.

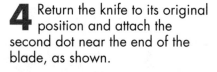

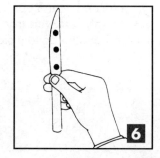

COMMENTS AND SUGGESTIONS

As mentioned earlier, the Paddle Move is a classic sleight with many important uses in magic. Study the illustrations and practice the move until you can do it smoothly and almost without thinking. You will have learned an extremely valuable sleight that you will perform in many different effects as you progress through the wonderful world of magic.

DOTS MAGIC— IMPROMPTU VERSION

DOTS MAGIC, as just described, can also be performed in a completely impromptu situation when you do not have the commercial dots with you.

EFFECT

The effect is the same as in DOTS MAGIC, except that instead of dots, you cut or tear small squares of paper (a paper napkin works well) for use in the trick. The squares are attached to the knife by moistening them slightly using the tip of your finger to obtain a drop of water from your water glass and applying it to each square. The slightly dampened squares will adhere to the blade of the knife.

SECRET AND PREPARATION

If you have an opportunity to apply the three secret squares before the performance, you may utilize the same routine as described in DOTS MAGIC. If you do not have the time or opportunity to tear, moisten, and apply the three extra squares, just start the routine from Step 10, using a total of three squares for the trick.

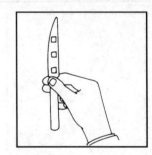

METHOD

1 Openly attach the three squares to one side of the examined blade.

2 Using the Paddle Move, show that three more identical squares have magically appeared on the opposite side of the blade.

3 Turn the blade over to show that the spots have vanished. Then use the Paddle Move to show the other side blank.

4 After showing both sides of the blade blank (again using the Paddle Move), the three squares reappear.

5 Proceed with Steps 11, 12, and 13, as the squares are openly removed from the top side of the blade and vanish from the bottom side.

GLASS THROUGH TABLE

EFFECT

You state that you will cause a solid object to penetrate through the top of the table. With that, you place a coin on the table and cover it with a glass, mouth down. You cover the glass with two paper napkins, concealing both the glass and coin from view. You explain that, by mere concentration, you will cause the coin to "melt" through the top of the table. After several unsuccessful attempts, you explain that the reason for failure is that you forgot one of the most important parts of the experiment. You must first strike the top of the glass, giving the coin the momentum to penetrate the table. Suddenly, with a sharp downward motion of your hand, you smash the glass and the napkins flat on the table. When the napkins are lifted, the coin is still there, but the glass is gone! Immediately, you reach beneath the table and produce the glass.

SECRET AND PREPARATION

The secret of this trick is based on a very clever principle. Due to the natural stiffness of the paper napkins, they will retain the form or shape of the glass even if the glass is not within them. This creates a very convincing illusion, making this mystery possible. The glass should be smooth-sided so it slides easily from within the napkins. It should also be slightly smaller at the base than at the mouth. A glass that is approximately 4" or 5" tall works well. In addition, you need a coin (a half-dollar is a good size) and two ordinary paper napkins.

METHOD

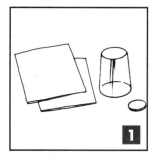

1 You must be seated at a card table or dining table to perform this close-up mystery. Also, it is better if the spectators are seated at the same table. With the glass, napkins, and coin lying on the table, tell the spectators that you will attempt to cause a solid object to pass through the top of the table.

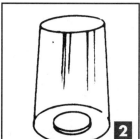

2 Place the coin directly in front of you, about 12" from the edge of the table. Cover the coin with the glass, mouth down. Point out that the glass completely encloses the coin so that it is impossible for you to touch it.

3 Open both napkins, lay them on top of each other, and place them over the glass, as shown. Explain that the coin must be kept in the dark, so you will cover the glass with the napkins.

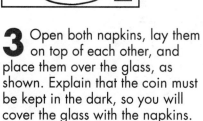

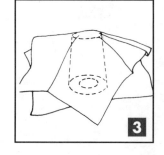

4 With both hands, pull the napkins downward around the glass. This makes the form of the glass clearly outlined through the napkins.

5 With one hand, grip the top of the glass through the napkins and place your other hand around the mouth of the glass. Then, twist the glass, as shown, drawing the napkins tightly against the sides of the glass. This helps to form the shape of the glass even more distinctly inside the paper napkins.

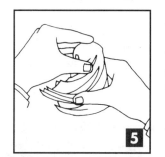

6 To reassure the spectators that the coin is still on the table, lift both the glass and the napkins together.

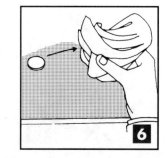

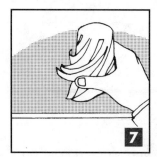

7 Once again, cover the coin with the glass and explain that through deep concentration you can cause the coin to penetrate through the table. All eyes will be fixed on the napkin-covered glass, waiting to see if the coin actually does as you say.

8 Pretend to concentrate for a few seconds. Then announce that you think the coin has done its work. With your right hand, lift the napkins and glass, revealing that the coin is still on the table. Act surprised, as if you actually expected the coin to be gone.

9 Pick up the coin in your left hand as you remark that something seems to be wrong. At the same time, move your right hand to the edge of the table, as shown, while holding the napkins and the glass. This motion of your right hand is completely natural, as it must move away to make room for your left hand, which picks up the coin. Your eyes, your gestures, your total attention should all be directed at the coin. This is misdirection!

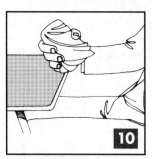

10 Here is a side view of the right hand holding the napkin-covered glass at the edge of the table. Notice that the hand is actually resting on the table.

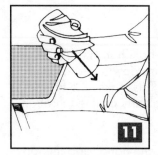

11 It is at this time that the secret move takes place. While the attention of the spectators is on the coin, the fingers of your right hand relax their grip on the glass through the napkins. The weight of the glass will cause it to slide from within the napkins into your lap.

12 The napkins retain the shape of the glass, creating the illusion that the glass is still there.

13 As the glass falls into your lap, raise your heels enough to bring your knees a bit higher than your lap. This keeps the glass in your lap, so it does not roll onto the floor.

14 Here is the spectators' view as the secret drop takes place. Notice how the left hand is forward, focusing attention on the coin.

15 Dropping the glass in your lap should take only a moment. As soon as the glass falls from the napkins, place the coin back on the table and cover it with the napkins (which apparently still contain the glass).

16 Explain that the trick failed because you forgot to strike the top of the glass. As you say this, raise your left hand above the glass.

17 Smash the napkins flat on the table with your left hand. When this is done fast and hard, the reaction from the spectators will be one of complete astonishment.

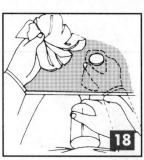

18 Act puzzled for a moment. Lift the napkins with your left hand, revealing the coin on the table. At the same time, your right hand grasps the glass in your lap and carries it beneath the table, as if reaching below the spot where you "smashed" the glass. Then bring your hand into view from beneath the table with the glass.

19 Place the glass on the table and say, "Now I remember how the trick is done! It's the glass that is supposed to penetrate the table, not the coin."

SERPENTINE SILK I

EFFECT

You display a colorful silk handkerchief that you twirl into a loose, rope-like configuration. You tie a knot in its center. Holding the handkerchief at one end, you cause the handkerchief to visibly untie itself right before the disbelieving eyes of the spectators.

SECRET AND PREPARATION

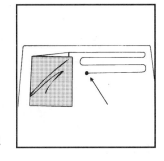

You will need a silk scarf or magician's silk handkerchief approximately 18" to 36" square and a spool of fine black nylon or silk thread. To prepare, attach one end of a 6' length of thread to one corner of the silk handkerchief. In the illustrations that follow, this corner has been labeled A and the free end of the handkerchief is marked B. The other end of the thread must be securely fastened to the top of your table (a small thumb tack works well). Fold the handkerchief and place it on your table, making sure that the thread is coiled next to the handkerchief, as shown in the illustration. You are now ready to present this classic mystery.

METHOD

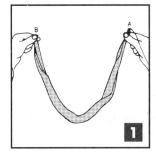

1 Pick up the folded handkerchief and stand approximately 3' in front of the table edge. Grasp Corner A in your right fingers and allow the silk to unfold in front of you. The thread should now be hanging at your right side, below your right arm. Reach down and grasp the bottom of the handkerchief, Corner B, in your left hand and twirl the handkerchief into a loose, rope-like configuration, as shown. The thread now runs across the top of your right thumb and under your right arm to the table top.

2 Bring End A across and over End B, as shown. As you do this, move your right hand so that the thread is held in position under your right thumb.

3 With your left hand, reach through the loop formed by the handkerchief.

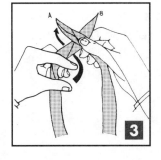

4 Grasp End A (and the thread) with the tops of your left fingers. Pull End A back through the loop.

5 Slowly and steadily draw your hands apart, forming a loose knot in the middle of the handkerchief. The thread sewn to Corner A will be drawn through the knot and should now run over your right thumb, as shown.

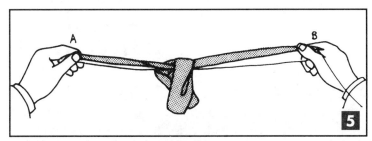

6 Release Corner A and allow the handkerchief to hang from your right hand. If you have performed all the steps correctly, the situation will be as follows: The thread, which is attached to Corner A, runs up and through the knot in the handkerchief.

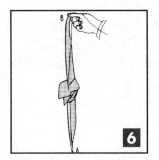

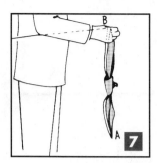

7 From there, it travels up and over your right thumb and under your right arm to the table.

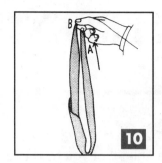

10 By moving your body slightly forward, the thread will pull the rest of the End A portion of the handkerchief through the knot, causing it to visibly dissolve.

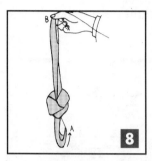

8 Hold the handkerchief close to your body and move forward just enough to remove any remaining slack in the thread. By extending your right arm, the thread will begin to pull End A upward, as shown.

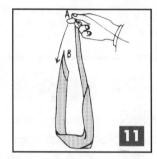

11 As soon as Corner A reaches your right fingers, immediately release Corner B, let it fall from your hand, and grasp Corner A.

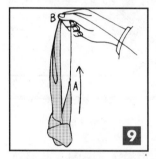

9 As you move your arm farther from the table, End A will be drawn into and completely through the knot, as shown.

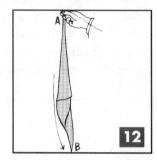

12 You now hold the "untied" handkerchief by Corner A with Corner B hanging below, as shown.

COMMENTS AND SUGGESTIONS

It will appear to the spectators that the handkerchief has a life of its own and has wiggled out of its own knot. The position of the handkerchief at the end of the sequence leaves you all set to repeat the effect. This happens to be one of the rare cases in magic where repetition will help to build the mystery, but it is best to repeat the effect only once. At the conclusion, simply crumple the handkerchief and drop it on your table.

SERPENTINE SILK II

You may wish to try the SERPENTINE SILK by this alternate method. Use a shorter length of thread with a small plastic bead tied to the free end. The end with the thread does not run to the table, as in the previous method. In this method, after the knot is tied the bead is secretly held under your right foot. The tying of the knot is the same as before, as is the action of the untying of the knot, except that this time you lift your arm instead of moving it forward. The benefit of this method is that you do not have to rely on a hookup to your table. With the bead-under-the-foot method, you can work the trick anywhere without fear of spoiling your setup. You will, however, need a bit more distance from the spectators, as the thread is more visible since it is not hidden by your body.

CHAPTER 2

ROPE MAGIC

Rope magic is an increasingly popular field for many magicians. One reason is that ropes are common objects, familiar to all. And when you cut one piece of ordinary rope or string into two pieces and then put it back together again, indeed you must be a magician of the highest rank.

But there are several other reasons for the popularity of rope magic. Ropes are easily rolled up and carried around discreetly. Simple close-up rope tricks can be performed anytime and anywhere in an impromptu fashion. Rope magic can be presented and seen in almost any setting. You can stand on a stage, a box, or a tree stump at a picnic and perform your rope miracles.

Ropes are also inexpensive. Most rope tricks are done with "magician's rope"—soft cotton rope that can be found at hardware stores. Magician's rope is also available from any magicians' supply store or mail-order company.

Although there is an end to every rope, there seems to be no end to the popularity of rope tricks. That is why you will find this section of very special value.

ROPE PREPARATION

In performing rope magic, there are several tips you should know about the preparation of the rope to achieve the most effective results in practice and presentation.

CORING

In certain tricks it is important that the rope be extremely flexible, even more so than it already is. To create this flexibility, you can do what is known as "coring" with many types of rope, especially the soft cotton rope used by magicians. If you look at the end of some types of rope, you will notice that the rope is constructed of a woven outer shell which contains an inner core. This core is made up of a number of individual cotton strands running the entire length of the rope.

To remove the core, cut off a piece of rope and spread open the threads of the outer shell at one end. With your fingers, firmly grasp the strands of cord that make up the core. With your other hand, get a firm hold on the outer shell near the same end and start pulling the core from within the rope's outer shell. As you pull the core and slide the outer shell, you will find that the shell tends to bunch up and then bind, making it difficult to pull out the inner core. When this happens, grasp the rope just below the bunched up shell and pull the shell down along the length of the remaining core until the shell is straight again, with the empty shell extending from the other end of the core. Then pull another length of core out from within the shell until it binds again. Continue this process of pulling and unbunching until the core has been completely removed from within the shell of rope. You can discard the core. This leaves you with the soft, flexible outer shell of the rope. To the spectators, however, the rope will appear just the same as before you removed the core.

FIXING THE ENDS

Another suggestion that will aid in maintaining the appearance of your rope, particularly if it has been cored, is to permanently "fix" the ends of the rope so that they will not fray (come apart). This can be done in several ways.

1 A particularly good method is to dip the end of the rope into a small amount of white glue and allow it to dry overnight. This will permanently bond all the loose fibers together and prevent them from unraveling.

2 Wax or paraffin also works well for this purpose. After melting the wax, dip the ends of the rope into the liquid wax and allow them to dry. This method has the advantage of a short drying period. Your ropes can be prepared only minutes before a performance.

3 Another method that works well is to tie off the ends of the rope with regular, white sewing thread after the rope has been cut to the desired length. Simply wrap the thread around the ends of the rope and tie the ends tightly to keep the rope from unwinding.

4 One final method is to wrap a small piece of white adhesive tape or transparent cellophane tape around the ends of the rope. Because tape is more visible, however, it may draw undue attention to the ends of the rope and distract from the effect being presented. The tape method is a good, fast way to get your rehearsal ropes ready.

DOUBLE-WALLED BAG

As the title suggests, this is not a trick in itself. It is rather a prop that will be very useful to you as a utility piece of equipment for switching one item for another or as a complete "vanish" for small objects. The strong point of this special bag is that it can be torn open after completing an effect to show that it is empty.

SECRET AND PREPARATION

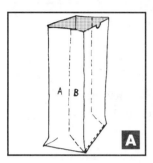

A Acquire two identical paper bags. (Two brown lunch bags are perfect.) Cut one of the bags along the dotted line, as shown. Save Part B and discard Part A.

B Spread Part B flat on the table and apply glue along the three edges, as shown.

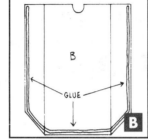

C Carefully slide Part B into the unprepared bag and align the top edges of both bags. Press the glued edges of Part B to the bottom and sides of the unprepared bag. The edges of Part B are glued to the same matching parts of the inside of the unprepared bag.

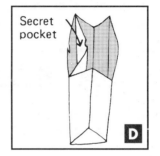

D You now have an ordinary-looking paper bag, but you have added an undetectable secret pocket.

E Before using it in a trick, the bag should be folded flat. When you are ready to use it, just pick up the flat bag and open it. This helps give the spectators the impression that it is just an ordinary paper bag. At the conclusion of the effect, you can tear away the unprepared side so that the spectators can see clearly into the bag. Make sure to keep the prepared side closed by holding it at the top edge with your hand. One of the many uses of the bag will be explained in the following effect.

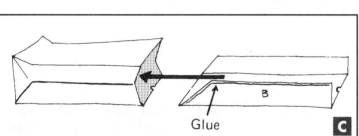

COMEDY
CUT-AND-RESTORED ROPE

EFFECT

You give a spectator a piece of rope approximately 3' long. Have the spectator cut the rope into two equal parts. After viewing the result, you decide to have the spectator cut the two pieces again, making four equal parts. Taking the four pieces of rope, you drop them one by one into an empty paper bag. You close the top of the bag and shake it vigorously. You tell the spectator that by waving the scissors over the bag, the rope will mysteriously restore itself to one piece. Upon opening the bag, the spectator sees that the rope has restored itself, but not in the way you had intended. Instead of one piece, the rope has magically tied itself together with three equally spaced knots. The bag is shown to be empty and is tossed aside. In order to solve this new problem, you simply give the end of the tied rope a sharp pull. The three knots fly off the rope, leaving it completely restored!

SECRET AND PREPARATION

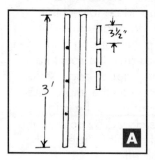

A Cut two 3' lengths of soft rope and three short pieces of rope about 3½" long. These short lengths will be used to form the fake knots that later pop off the rope. Stretch out one of the long pieces of rope and mark it lightly with a pencil in quarters, as shown. These marks show you where to attach the fake knots that apparently divide the rope into four equal parts.

B To tie the fake knots, fold the long rope at one of the three pencil marks.

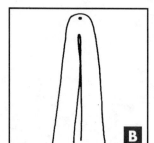

C and **D** Tie one of the short pieces of rope around the folded rope, as shown.

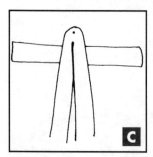

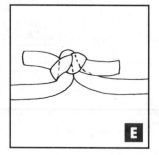

E When you straighten the long rope, the knot will appear like this. If you pull on the rope, the knot will pop off.

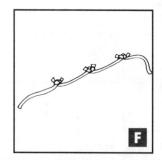

F Tie the other two short pieces around the other two marked spots on the long rope. You now appear to have one long piece of rope made up of three short pieces knotted together.

G You will need a DOUBLE-WALLED BAG (see page 35). Open the bag and place the prepared rope into the main compartment, as shown. Do not place it into the secret pocket, as this area will be used to conceal the cut pieces later in the routine. Fold the bag flat and put it on your table.

METHOD

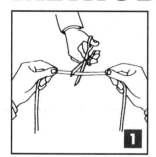

1 Invite a spectator to join you in teaching a trick. Hand this person the scissors and display the 3' rope. Instruct the spectator to cut the rope in half.

2 Have the spectator cut the rope again, this time into four equal parts.

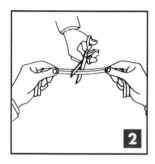

3 Pick up the paper bag and open it. Be careful not to show the inside of the bag, or you will expose the presence of the prepared rope. Drop the four pieces of rope, one at a time, into the secret compartment of the bag.

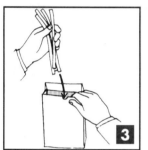

4 Close the top of the bag and shake it so that the spectator can hear the rope inside. Tell the spectator to wave the scissors over the bag, and the rope will restore itself "as if by magic."

5 Reach into the main compartment of the bag and remove the prepared rope (the one with the fake knots). Be sure to keep the secret pocket closed while you do this.

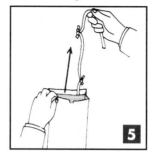

6 Place the knotted rope aside and tear open the front of the bag to show that it is empty. (The cut pieces remain concealed in the secret pocket.) Set the bag aside and explain that the spectator almost made it, but it looks as if you will have to finish the trick.

7 Hold both ends of the prepared rope between your hands, as shown.

8 Pull sharply on the ends of the rope, causing the fake knots to fly off the rope into the air. The rope has been restored!

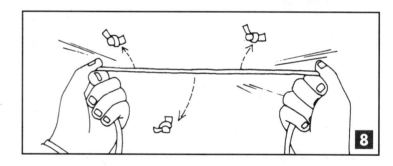

TRIPLE ROPE TRICK

This differs from a cut-and-restore trick because no actual cutting is done. Instead, you start with three short lengths of rope and magically form them into a single, long rope. One particular advantage to this mystery is that no scissors are needed, so you can carry the ropes in your pocket and work the trick anytime, anywhere.

EFFECT

You show three pieces of rope that are about equal in length, pointing out that all three are knotted together at both ends. You untie one group of three knotted ends and then retie two of the ropes together again. Next you untie the other group of three knotted ends, and retie two of these ropes together. This leaves the three ropes tied end to end, forming one long rope—except for the knots! You coil the rope around one hand and remove a half-dollar from your pocket, which you wave over the rope. When the rope is uncoiled, the knots have vanished, and the three short ropes have amazingly turned into one single length that can be tossed to the spectators for examination.

SECRET AND PREPARATION

Actually, one long rope and two short pieces are used. The long rope is about 3' in length; the short pieces are each about 4" long. The preparation for this trick is as follows.

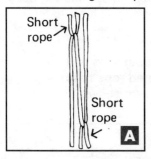

Short rope
Short rope

A Lay out the long rope in three sections. Loop a short piece of rope in the two bends of the long piece, as shown.

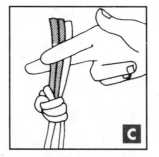

B Tie the three upper ends (one end of the long rope and two ends of the short rope) into one single knot, as shown. To the spectators, these appear to be the ends of three single ropes. Only you know that two of the ends are from the short rope and the third is one end of the long rope.

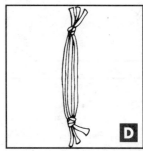

C This is how the knot looks when pulled tight.

D Tie the other three ends together in exactly the same way. This is all prepared ahead of time. To the spectators, it appears that you have three lengths of rope with their ends tied together.

METHOD

1 Display the "three ropes" to the spectators. With both hands, untie the large knot at one end. Make sure not to reveal that two of the ends are from the short piece of rope.

2 Hold the ropes in your left hand between your thumb and fingers, as shown. Your left thumb clips the short loop above where the long rope loops over the short rope, concealing it from view with your left fingers.

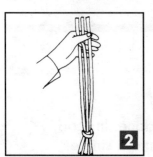

3 Let the end of the long rope drop, so that you are holding only the two ends of the short piece and the looped-over part of the long rope.

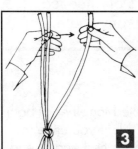

4 After you drop the long end, the rope should look like this.

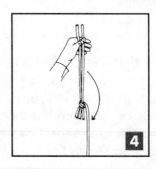

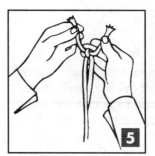

5 Tie the short rope in a single knot around the long rope. Say, "I will tie two of the ropes together." Be sure to keep the small loop hidden by your fingers until the knot is tied. After that it can be freely shown.

6 Grasp the remaining large knot and repeat Steps 1 through 5. Say, "Now I will tie these two pieces of rope together as well."

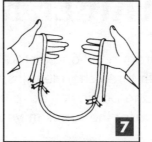

7 Show what appears to be three short ropes knotted to form a single long one. Actually, it is one long rope with two short ropes tied to look like connecting knots.

8 Hold one end of the rope in your left hand and begin coiling the rope around your left hand with your right hand. As you wrap it around, the rope naturally slides through your right hand. When you come to the first knot, keep it in your right hand, secretly slipping it along the rope.

9 When you come to the second knot, slide it along in the same way with your right hand. The spectators will think that the knots are still on the rope coiled around your left hand.

12 Make a magical wave of the coin over the rope and replace the coin in your pocket. Unwind the rope from your hand, showing the knots completely gone!

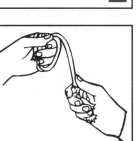

10 As you complete the coiling, secretly slide both knots off the end of the rope.

11 Remark that you will now use your "magic coin." Your right hand goes into your right pocket—where you leave the knots and bring out the half-dollar.

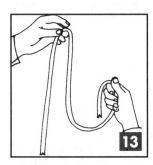

13 The three short ropes have been magically transformed into one single, long rope—much to the amazement of the spectators!

COMMENTS AND SUGGESTIONS

The strong point of this clever mystery is that the trick is actually done before you begin. Therefore, you should stress that you have three single ropes at the start.

TRIPLE ROPE— MULTIPLE "DO AS I DO" KNOT

With receptive spectators, you can amplify this effect by giving out three sets of knotted ropes, letting two spectators follow along with you. Again, your ropes come out as one long piece and theirs do not. That is why it is called the "DO AS I DO" KNOT.

METHOD

1 In using three sets (one special and two regular), the selection procedure is simple and neat. If both spectators (let's call them Joe and Anne) take an ordinary set, you keep the special one and proceed with your routine, having them copy your moves.

2 However, if Joe happens to take the special set, say, "You can see that your three ropes are knotted together at both ends." Then, take your set and give it to Joe, saying, "Take my ropes and give yours to Anne." As Joe gives the special set to Anne, take the ordinary set that Anne is holding. Continue, ". . . so Anne can give her ropes to me."

3 Briefly look at the set you took from Anne, then give it to Joe, saying, "Now take Anne's ropes and give her mine." As Joe does that, take the special set that Anne has, saying, "And Anne, give me yours." Then, speaking to both of them, you say, "Now that we have each checked all three sets of ropes to see that they are exactly alike, I want each of you to do exactly as I do."

COMMENTS AND SUGGESTIONS

In winding the coils around your left hand, be sure to tell your helpers to coil each knot inside the left hand, just as you do. Then go through the motion of bringing invisible "magic powder" from your pocket and tell them to do the same. The only difference is that your powder works, while theirs doesn't. This is proven when you each uncoil your rope and you have one long, single length, free of knots, while theirs haven't changed at all. You can also explain that your magic powder is truly invisible, whereas theirs is purely imaginary.

TRIPLE ROPE—
"TIMES TWO"

This is a special form of presentation for the TRIPLE ROPE trick, especially suited for small or intimate gatherings. It falls into the category of a "Do As I Do" effect, making it an ideal addition to the spectator-participation portion of your program.

SECRET AND PREPARATION

This time start with two sets of knotted ropes. One is the special type already described: one long rope with two short loops, each looped to a portion of the long rope and knotted there to show three ends. The second set consists of three separate ropes, about the same length. These are actually knotted at both ends, so they look exactly the same as your fake set. You can identify the special set by making a small ink or pencil mark on one of the knots. The mark should be just large enough for you to notice.

METHOD

1 Bring out both sets of knotted ropes, remarking that each consists of three short ropes knotted at both ends. Explain that you intend to use one set in this mystery and the spectator is to use the other. Also explain that since both are exactly alike, the spectator may choose either set.

2 If the spectator takes the ordinary set, you keep the special set and say, "I want you to do exactly as I do. Untie your ropes like this." With that, you proceed step-by-step as already described with the "three in one" effect.

3 If the spectator takes the special set, the one that you should have, you can handle the situation quite easily. Say, "Good, now I want you to do just as I do. Give me your three ropes, so I can untie their ends, while I give you my three ropes, so you can untie them." Thus the exchange of ropes becomes the first step in the "Do As I Do" procedure, and you simply carry on from there.

4 Proceed with the step-by-step process, moving slowly and deliberately so the spectator can copy your moves exactly. Since everyone sees that the spectator has three separate ropes, they will assume that yours are the same.

5 On the last step, you wrap the rope around your hand and then reach into your pocket to remove some invisible "magic dust." Tell the spectator, who has been duplicating your every move, to pretend to have a pocketful and to sprinkle it on the rope as you do the same. (It is at this point that you leave the two knots in your pocket.) Your rope now comes out all in one piece while the spectator's is still in three pieces—proving that there is no substitute for "real" invisible magic dust. Give the spectator a handful from your pocket along with the unrestored rope!

CUT-AND-RESTORED STRING

The following is one of those clever effects that can be presented anywhere and always leaves the spectators completely baffled. It might well be classified as a close-up version of the more familiar cut-and-restore rope tricks. However, the method for this effect is quite different, which makes the mystery all the more puzzling.

EFFECT

You call attention to a single length of string that you proceed to cut into two equal parts. You give one end of each of the cut strings to a spectator to hold. With everything in full view, the spectator instantly restores the twine to its original condition. The stunned spectator is then given the piece of string as a souvenir.

SECRET AND PREPARATION

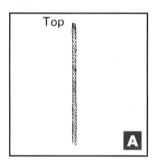

A The secret of this trick depends on a very clever principle. The properties of a certain type of common string are so obvious they go totally unnoticed by everyone. This type of string is composed of many individual strands of twine twisted together to form a multi-stranded string. It is sometimes referred to as "butcher's twine." It is usually thicker than ordinary string (like kite string) and is soft and white in color. To perform this mystery, all you need is a length of this type of string approximately 18" long. For the purpose of explanation, we will refer to the ends of the string as X and Y.

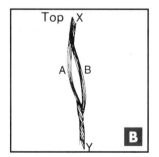

B Locate the center of the piece of string and spread the individual strands open, dividing the string into two equal sections of twine. We will refer to these sections as A and B.

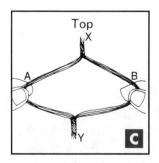

C Pull Sections A and B about 5" apart, as shown. Slowly roll each section between your fingers so that they twist together to form two new false ends.

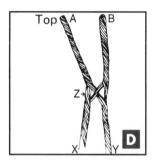

D Adjust the entire affair so that the two newly formed string ends (AX and BY) run so close together at the place where they connect (Point Z) that the secret connection between them is nearly impossible to detect.

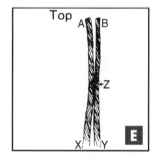

E At this point, A and B form two fake ends of string, and X and Y (the real ones), the other ends. It appears that you have two separate strings.

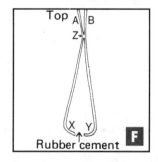

F Apply a very small dab of rubber cement to Ends X and Y and allow them to become nearly dry. Then, attach the two ends (X and Y) together by rolling them between your fingers until they are joined.

G The resulting product should look like one continuous length of string, as shown. If this is done correctly, the string can be handled quite casually as you display it during the presentation.

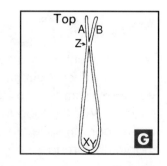

METHOD

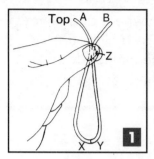

1 Display the prepared string, casually calling attention to the fact that you hold only one piece of string. As you prepare to cut the string, adjust your grip so that you hold it between the tops of your left fingers, as shown here. Your thumb and first finger should cover the secret connection (Z).

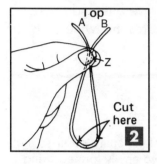

2 With scissors, cut the string (both pieces) near the bottom of the hanging loop just above Point XY. Let the glued joint (XY) drop to the floor, leaving you two new unglued X and Y ends. This automatically removes the only gimmicked part of the string for the astonishing conclusion of the trick.

3 Call attention to the absolute fairness of every move you make. The spectators will be convinced that you have merely cut a single length of twine into two equal parts.

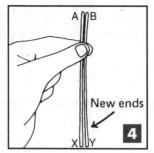

4 Place the scissors aside and display the two separate pieces of string. Be sure to handle the string(s) in a casual manner so as not to give the impression that you are concealing something, but keep the strings together at the secret connection (Z).

5 Ask a spectator to grasp Ends X and Y. When this is done, you hold Ends A and B (and the secret connection Z) in your closed fist, as shown.

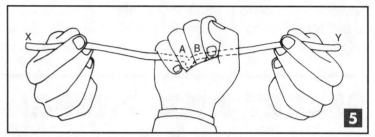

6 Tell the spectator to pull sharply on the ends in opposite directions. When the spectator does this, release your grip on the string. Allow the secret connection to untwist and thus restore itself to its original form—the center of the string! All of the spectators will be astonished to see the strings weld themselves together as the ends are pulled.

COMMENTS AND SUGGESTIONS

Stress the fact that the string actually restores itself while the spectator holds both ends. The beautiful thing here is that there are no secret gimmicks or extra pieces of string to get rid of. As you can see, this is another outstanding close-up mystery. Build it up properly and you will be credited with performing a small miracle.

THREADING THE NEEDLE

EFFECT

You call attention to an ordinary piece of soft rope that is approximately 3' in length. You explain that even under the most adverse circumstances it is easy to magically thread a needle, if you know the secret. To demonstrate, you form a small loop from one end of the rope to represent the eye of a needle; the other end will substitute for the thread. With the loop in your left hand and the thread end of the rope in your right hand, you make a quick thrust at the loop. In spite of your speed and the fact that you may not even come near the loop, the needle has been magically threaded!

METHOD

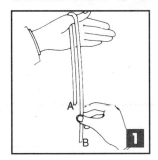

1 After displaying the rope to the spectators, lay the rope over your left thumb so that Length A will measure approximately 12" and Length B will measure about 24".

2 Grasp Length B with your right hand and wrap the rope around your left thumb twice. Be sure you wrap the rope around your thumb in the direction shown in the illustration.

3 With your right hand, grasp Length B and twist the rope to form a loop about 2" high, as shown. This loop is lifted and placed between your left thumb and forefinger.

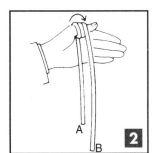

4 Grip the loop between your left thumb and forefinger so that it protrudes over the top of the thumb. This loop now represents the eye of the needle. End B of the rope must be the side of the loop closest to the palm of your left hand, as shown by the dotted lines in the illustration.

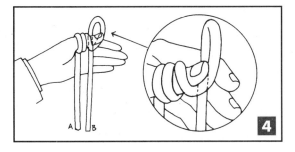

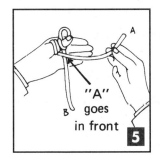

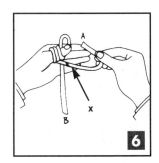

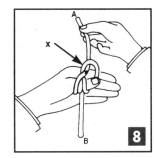

5 End A will now become the thread. Grasp A with your right thumb and fingers about 1" from the end. Lift A in front of B and hold, as shown.

6 Steps 6 and 7 are the actual threading. With End A in your right hand, move that hand forward, missing the loop with the end but allowing the lower part of A (marked with an "X" in the illustration) to pass between the left thumb and left fingers.

7 As Length A passes between the left thumb and the left fingers, loosen your grip slightly by relaxing the left thumb as you pull Length A up sharply with the right hand.

8 The X part of Length A will now be through the loop, and it will appear as if you have threaded the eye without even coming close with the thread.

NOTE: There is now one less turn of rope around your left thumb. You lose one of these turns each time you thread the needle.

9 If you unthread the needle by really pulling End A back through the loop, you can immediately thread it again. (Notice again that there is one less turn around your left thumb.)

COMMENTS AND SUGGESTIONS

This effect is excellent when used in combination with other rope tricks to create an entertaining rope routine. On its own it also makes a good challenge at a party, for no matter how hard the spectators try to duplicate your movements, they will find it impossible to thread the eye of the needle.

When using the effect as a spectator challenge, be sure that the spectator attempts the threading using Length B as the thread. By substituting B for A, the trick becomes impossible to duplicate. You will also find, during practice, that you will be able to move your right hand as fast as you wish and still thread the needle because the end of the thread never actually passes through the needle anyway.

ONE-HAND KNOT

EFFECT

You display a 3' length of soft rope. Casually tossing the rope into the air, a genuine knot appears magically in its center.

METHOD

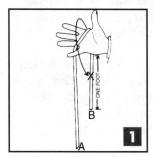

1 Display a length of rope—a piece about 3' long is best. Drape it over your right hand, with End A hanging between the third and fourth fingers and End B between your thumb and first finger. Although End A may be any length, End B must not fall more than about 1' below your hand.

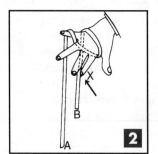

2 Turn your right hand over and grasp Length B between the first and second fingers at "AX," as shown.

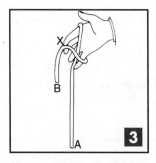

3 Rotate your hand back up, as shown, holding B firmly between the first and second fingers.

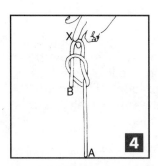

4 Simply allow the loop that has been formed around your right hand to fall off your hand.

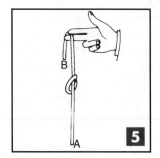

5 The end of B will be drawn through this loop, forming a knot in the rope. You may also snap the rope off your hand rather than letting it fall.

COMMENTS AND SUGGESTIONS

In order to disguise what is actually happening, practice the following movement: After grasping Length B firmly with the first and second fingers of the right hand (Step 2), throw the rope straight up into the air, letting go of Length B after it has passed through the loop. The effect will be that the knot was tied in the air.

NOTE: The softer the rope, the easier it is to do this trick. It will also work equally well with a soft handkerchief (silk is best) of the proper size.

MELTING KNOT

EFFECT

You slowly and deliberately tie a knot in the center of a 3' piece of rope. The spectators watch as you gradually tighten the knot by pulling on both ends of the rope. The knot becomes smaller until, just before cinching up tight, it melts away into nothingness!

SECRET AND PREPARATION

Once again, you will have use for that 3' length of soft rope. This mystery, combined with THREADING THE NEEDLE and other such effects, makes an entertaining routine with just this short length of rope.

METHOD

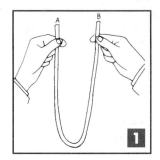

1 Display the rope to the spectators. (In the illustrations, we will call the end in your left hand End A and the one in your right End B.)

2 With your right hand, bring End B around behind your left hand and over the top of End A. Place End B between your left first and second fingers and release your right hand. You should now be hiding the rope, as shown.

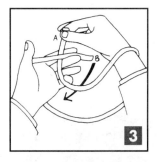

3 Pass your right hand through the loop of rope and grasp End A between your right thumb and first finger.

4 Pull Ends A and B apart. Hold End B with your left thumb and fingers. As you do this, pull End A through the loop and slowly separate your hands.

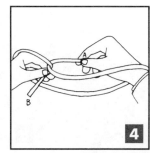

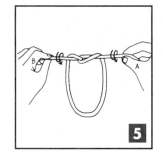

5 You have now formed a false knot. In order to keep the knot from dissolving prematurely, you must roll or twist the rope with the thumb and first finger of each hand. Roll or twist the rope in the direction shown by the arrows (toward yourself).

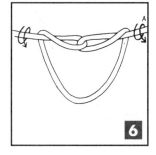

6 You can clearly see the reasons for twisting the rope here. The rolling action of the ends forces the false knot to ride up and over itself, thus maintaining its knot shape.

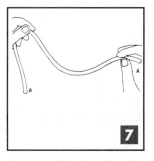

7 When the knot is just about to tighten up, blow on it as you pull the ends. The knot seems to dissolve into thin air. Properly preformed, the illusion is so perfect that you may immediately repeat the trick without fear of discovery.

SHOELACE ROPE TIE

EFFECT

You display a 3′ length of soft rope to the spectators. Holding it between both hands, you skillfully tie a bow knot in the rope. You then thread the ends of the rope through the loops of the bows and pull the ends so that a hopeless knot is formed in the center of the rope. The spectators understand your problem, for they have probably had this happen with their shoelaces many times. However, as if to defy the laws of nature, you cause the cumbersome knot to dissolve before the eyes of the spectators!

METHOD

All you need for this clever effect is a soft rope approximately 3′ in length.

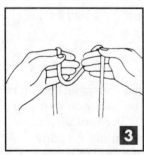

1 Display the rope to the spectators and then lay it across the fingers of your right and left hands, as shown. Your left hand is above your right hand, your palms face you, and the backs of your hands are toward the spectators.

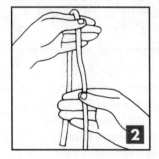

2 Hold the rope in position by pressing your thumbs against the rope.

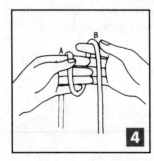

3 Move your right hand next to your left hand, allowing the rope to hook underneath the left fingers and over the top of the right fingers.

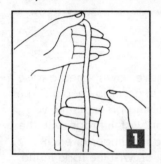

4 Move your right hand behind your left hand, as shown.

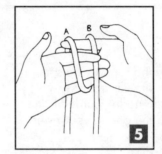

5 Clip the rope at Point A between the tips of your right first and second fingers. At the same time, grasp the rope at Point B with your left first and second fingers. (Study the illustration carefully.)

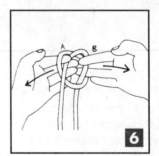

6 Hold the two points (A and B) tightly between the fingers of each hand and begin to draw your hands apart.

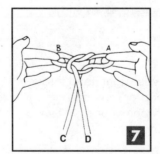

7 As you continue to pull your hands apart, a bow knot will begin to form in the middle of the rope.

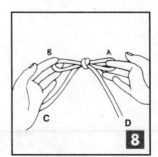

8 Gently pull the completed "bow knot" taut, as shown.

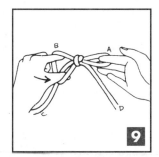

9 With your left thumb and first finger, reach through the left bow (B) and grasp the left end of the rope (C).

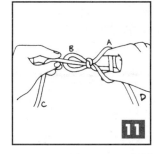

10 Pull the left end of the rope (C) back through the loop.

11 With your right thumb and first finger, reach through the right-hand bow (A) and grasp the right-hand end of the rope (D).

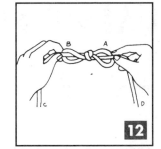

12 Pull that end of the rope (D) back through the loop (A).

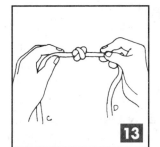

13 Release the bows and gently pull on the ends of the rope, causing the bow to cinch up and form a large knot in the center of the rope. If you have followed the steps correctly, this knot will actually be a slipknot, or dissolving knot, as magicians often call it. Do not pull too hard on the ends or you will dissolve the knot too soon!

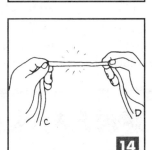

14 Instead, display the knot to the spectators as you comment about how bothersome a situation like this can be when it happens in everyday life. You might remark, "Being a magician comes in handy when this happens because all you have to do is to use the old 'knot-vanishing move' to get out of trouble." As you say this, pull on the ends of the rope, and the knot will magically vanish.

COMMENTS AND SUGGESTIONS

At first, when you start learning this clever effect, it may seem complicated and difficult to follow. Study the pictures carefully. The tying of the bow and the pulling of the ends through the loops will be perfectly natural and easy. These actions can be accompanied by clever patter, perhaps about how you became interested in magic as a child when you found that, in tying your shoes, the ends of the laces would slip through the bows and you always ended up with a knot. But when you began to study magic, you discovered that by merely pulling on the ends of the laces and blowing on the knot at the same time (or saying the magic words), the knot would dissolve itself.

EQUAL-UNEQUAL ROPES

EFFECT

You display four lengths of rope by holding two ropes in each hand. Each pair is tied together in the center so that they form two sets of two ropes each. One of these sets consists of one long piece of rope and one short piece, while the other set contains two ropes exactly the same length. You ask for two spectators to come up on the stage. Each is then given one set of ropes. The spectator on the right, who holds the long and the short pair of ropes, is asked to turn around and face away from the audience. You pin one short and one long piece of ribbon on the back of this spectator to identify the sets of ropes. The spectator on the left, who holds the two equal ropes, is also asked to turn around and is marked by attaching two equal pieces of ribbon on their back. You point out that the ribbons enable the audience to easily identify the location of each set of ropes, even when the backs of the spectators are facing them. You then have both spectators face the audience as you explain that you will cause something magical to happen. With that, you ask them to again turn their backs to the audience and to untie their pairs of ropes. This done, they are asked to turn around and face the audience to show the ropes that they hold. To the surprise of the audience, as well as the two spectators, the two equal lengths of rope have magically exchanged positions with the two unequal pieces of rope!

SECRET AND PREPARATION

This clever mystery can be classified as a self-working trick, as the entire trick takes place in the hands of the spectators. The secret lies in the clever manner in which you have knotted the ropes before the show. For the trick, all you need are three pieces of soft rope about 5' in length, one piece of rope exactly half that long, and some ribbon.

A To prepare, place two of the 5' lengths side by side, as shown. For the purpose of explanation, the ropes have been labeled A and B and, for clarity only, are shown in different colors. When performing the trick, all of the ropes must be the same color.

C Fold both ends of Rope B together, so that they run side by side in the same direction. Do the same with the ends of Rope A, as shown in this illustration.

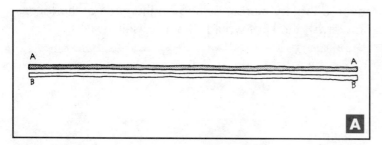

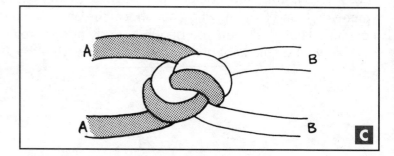

B Tie the two ropes together with a single overhand knot at a point approximately one-third of the distance from the end, as illustrated.

D Tie another overhand knot on top of the first knot to further confuse the spectators. The result will appear to be one long and one short piece of rope tied together at the center.

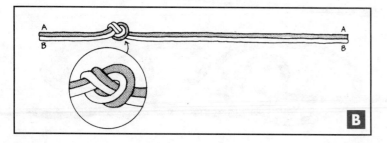

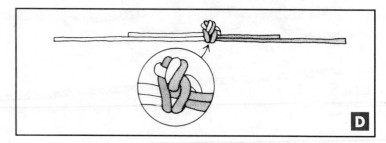

E The next step is to tie the two unequal lengths of rope together so that they look as if they are equal in length. To do this, place the short piece (C) next to the long piece (D). The short rope (C) must be centered between the ends of the long rope (D).

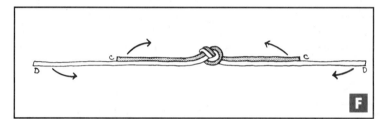

F Tie the ropes together in the center using a single overhand knot, as shown.

G Bring both ends of the short rope (C) together so they run side by side and do the same with the ends of the long rope (D). Secure the ends in place with another overhand knot. The result will appear to be two equal pieces of rope tied together at their centers.

H Finally, you will need three pieces of colorful ribbon about 2' long, and a fourth piece about 1' long. Attach a small pin to the end of each ribbon, and you are ready to present EQUAL-UNEQUAL ROPES.

METHOD

1 Display the two sets of ropes as you ask for the assistance of two spectators.

2 Give the spectator to your right the set of ropes that appears to be the unequal lengths (actually the equal ropes). To the spectator on your left, give the set that appears to be two equal lengths.

3 Have both spectators turn their backs to the audience and attach the corresponding lengths of ribbon to their coats. Have them turn back to face the audience as you explain that the ribbons will serve to identify which spectator holds which set of ropes.

4 Instruct the spectators to again turn their backs to the audience and then to untie their ropes. If you wish, you can now say something magical is going to happen. With that, instruct the spectators to turn and face the audience, holding one rope in each hand. Sure enough, when they turn around, the spectator on the left now has one short and one long rope instead of two of the same length, and the one on the right now has two ropes of the same length rather than two of unequal lengths. The two sets of ropes have magically exchanged positions while in the hands of the spectators!

COMMENTS AND SUGGESTIONS

This is a very clever novelty trick that always brings a laugh. Performed correctly, the two spectators themselves will not even get wise to the trick. Strange as it seems, when they untie these knots, the ropes seem to change length right in their hands, and they will not be able to understand how it happened! Of course, if you were to immediately repeat the trick, they would watch the ends and no doubt figure it out. However, the first time you work this, it will leave the spectators as mystified as the audience, enhancing the total effect.

RING OFF ROPE

There are various tricks involving rings and ropes, and this is one of the best. RING OFF ROPE has the impact of an impromptu effect when done at close range, yet it can also be performed before a fairly large group with the assistance of two spectators, making it an equally good item for your stage show.

EFFECT

You borrow a finger ring from a spectator. You ask another spectator to thread it on a rope about 3' in length. Two spectators hold the rope, one at each end, yet you cause the ring to magically penetrate right through the rope! The ring is immediately returned to its owner. The ring can be thoroughly examined, along with the length of rope.

METHOD

1 Hand a spectator a piece of rope about 3' long for examination as you ask to borrow a finger ring from another. Retrieve the examined rope and invite a third spectator to thread the borrowed ring on the rope. Next, invite two spectators to help you with the trick. Ask one to stand to the left of you, and the other to the right.

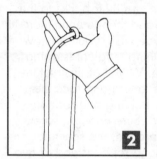

2 Lay the threaded ring and rope across your upturned right hand. The ring should rest near the base of your first finger, and the ends of the rope should hang down from both sides of your hand, as shown.

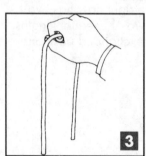

3 As you display the rope in this manner, remark that it would be impossible to remove the ring from the rope without sliding it off one of the ends. With that, close your fingers over the ring and turn your hand completely over so that the back of your hand is up. The ring should be held loosely by your first finger near the very edge of your hand, as shown.

4 This illustration is a close-up view of how the ring should be held in your hand.

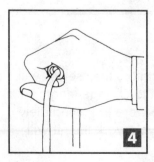

NOTE: To conceal the ring from the view of the spectator on your left, you can move your right thumb upward to fill in the open space where the ring might be seen in your hand.

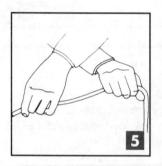

5 With the ring and rope held in this position, reach your left hand across your right forearm and grasp the dangling rope where it emerges from your right hand. Slide your left hand along the rope and give the right end of the rope to the spectator on that side. Ask the spectator to hold that end. (The illustration is from the spectators' viewpoint.)

6 After the spectator grasps the right end of the rope, slide your half-cupped left hand along the rope, bringing it beneath your right fist.

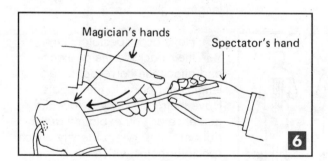

Magician's hands

Spectator's hand

7 At the very moment your left hand arrives below your fist, tilt your right hand slightly to the left and relax your right first finger. Allow the ring to secretly drop from your right fist into your left fingers.

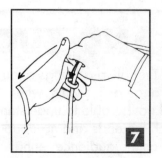

NOTE: This drop should be done smoothly and without hesitation. If your left hand pauses for even the slightest moment, you will tip-off the audience that something suspicious is happening. This is the key move for this trick.

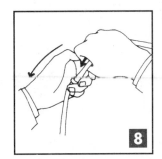

8 After your left hand catches the ring, raise your right hand upward. Look directly into the eyes of the spectator on your right and say, "Hold your end a little higher."

NOTE: This is a good example of the use of misdirection while the vital move of the trick takes place. By looking at and talking to the spectator, you take attention off the rope just long enough to make the secret steal. Also, by raising your right hand upward, the attention of the audience will be directed toward that hand, instead of your left hand, which secretly contains the ring.

Spectator's hand

Magician's hand

9 As you raise your right hand upward, your left hand (and the ring) slides down along the rope and secretly carries the ring completely off the end of the rope. Without hesitation, as you secretly hold the ring in the finger-palm position (see FINGER-PALM VANISH, page 70), lift this end and give it to the spectator on your left. Tell the spectator to hold the end firmly.

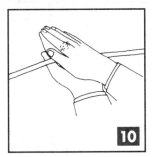

10 Bring your left hand up beneath your right fist. Quickly open both hands, placing your palms together so that the rope and the now free ring are trapped between them. Start to roll your hands back and forth as if to cause the ring to dissolve through the center of the rope.

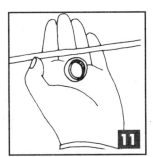

11 Lift your right hand to reveal the ring resting on your left hand next to the rope. Return the ring to its owner and pass the rope for examination.

COMMENTS AND SUGGESTIONS

Although using a borrowed ring is best, the routine is just as effective with your own finger ring, or even a small curtain ring or a metal washer. At the finish, everything can be examined, just as with the borrowed ring, so the effect on the audience is the same. The vital point is to make your presentation natural, so that no one will suspect the secret move. As you practice, working slowly and deliberately, you will find that the steal becomes easier and all the more deceptive. To condition the spectators to the naturalness of your actions, you can introduce the following before actually performing the trick: Hold the threaded ring in your open right palm as in Step 2. Say to the spectator on your right, "I am going to give you this end of the rope." With that, reach over with your left hand and start to give him the right end, but let it drop. Then say to the spectator on the left, "And I will give you this end," as you bring your left hand over and lift the left end of the rope and let it drop. Then say, "And all the while, I will keep the ring tightly in my right hand." With that, for the first time, turn your right fist downward. You are now all set to proceed, using almost the same moves with the ends of the rope, making the routine entirely natural throughout.

CHAPTER 3

MENTAL
SORCERY

Mental magic is unique because it depends upon the effect created on the audience rather than the objects used. Instead of making props vanish and reappear, or cutting them up and restoring them, you use them in special tests to presumably read people's minds.

Most mental effects depend upon some unsuspected secret that spectators are apt to overlook. In the following section, you will learn how to use these unsuspected secrets to make the audience believe that you have special mental powers. By emphasizing that these tricks are *tests* of your mental ability, not *tricks*, you will enhance your reputation and aura as a prestigious prestidigitator.

But please, don't take any of this too seriously. Remember, the goal of all magic is to entertain the audience by adding a bit of mystery and wonder to their day. Properly presented, Mental Sorcery will do just that.

MILLION TO ONE

EFFECT

You show the spectators ten small cards with a large spot printed on the face of each card. These cards are placed on the table in a long, straight row so that they alternate face up and face down. In this arrangement, the spectators can see five of the red spots and five of the red backs. You ask one of the spectators to think of the color blue. As soon as that is acknowledged, you ask the same person to call out a number between one and ten. With the number selected, you quickly point to the card that corresponds to the spectator's choice. To the complete surprise of your audience, this card proves to be the only blue card in the row.

SECRET AND PREPARATION

A The cards may be made from index cards or any type of stiff white cardboard. Use crayons or marking pens to color each card. Eight of the ten cards are alike. They all have a red spot on the face and red-colored backs.

B The two remaining cards are prepared differently. One card has a red spot on the face, but the back is colored blue. The other special card has a red back and a blue spot on the face.

C Arrange the ten cards in a stack. The top (uppermost) card is a regular card, face up. The second card from

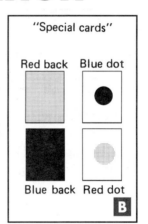

"Special cards"

Red back   Blue dot

Blue back   Red dot

B

the top is also regular, face down. The third card is the special blue-backed card, face up. The fourth card is the other special card with the blue dot, face down. The fifth card is regular, face up. The sixth card is regular, face down. The seventh card is regular, face up. The eighth card is regular, face down. The ninth card is regular, face up. The last card, the tenth card, is regular, face down.

METHOD

1 Using your left hand, hold the cards in the prearranged order. With your right hand, deal the ten cards, starting at the top of the packet, onto the table from left to right. This means that the cards alternate face up and face down and that the two special cards will be in the third and fourth positions from your left.

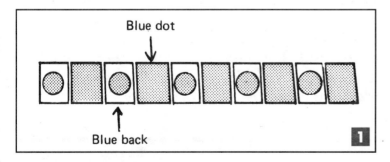

Blue dot

Blue back

1

2 After you have placed the cards on the table, ask a spectator to concentrate on the color "blue." Then, have that person call out any number between one and ten. You now proceed to force one of the two specially prepared (blue) cards on the spectator.

3 After hearing the spectator's number, count the cards. Here is the procedure for whatever number the spectator calls:

NUMBER ONE—Begin with the card at the left end and spell, "O, N, E," arriving at the third (blue-backed) card.

NUMBER TWO—Begin at the left end and spell, "T, W, O," arriving at the third (blue-backed) card.

NUMBER THREE—Count, "One, Two, Three," from the left arriving at the third (blue-backed) card.

NUMBER FOUR—Count, "One, Two, Three, Four," from the left, arriving at the fourth (blue-spotted) card.

NUMBER FIVE—Begin at the left and spell, "F, I, V, E," arriving at the fourth (blue-spotted) card.

NUMBER SIX—Begin at the left and spell, "S, I, X," arriving at the third (blue-backed) card.

NUMBER SEVEN—Have the spectator count from the right end of the row, arriving at the fourth (blue-spotted) card.

NUMBER EIGHT—Have the spectator count from the right end, arriving at the third (blue-backed) card.

NUMBER NINE—Begin at your left end and spell, "N, I, N, E," arriving at the fourth (blue-spotted) card.

NUMBER TEN—Begin at your left end and spell, "T, E, N," arriving at the third (blue-backed) card.

4 After you have finished the spelling or counting, emphasize the fact that the spectator was given a free choice of any card. (Or so the spectator thinks!) Turn the chosen (forced) card over to show that the opposite side is blue.

5 If the selected card is the blue-backed (third) card, turn all the cards that are face-up cards face down to show that all have red backs except the chosen card.

6 If the selected card is the blue-spotted (fourth) card, turn all the cards that are face down, face up to show that all have red spots except the chosen card.

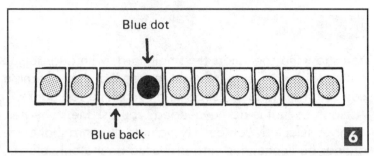

7 This final turning of the cards serves to convince the spectators that the cards are all identical except for the one card that the spectator selected, and to conceal the fact that you are using one more specially prepared card. After this turnover, gather up all the cards, being careful not to expose the remaining special (blue) card among the rest.

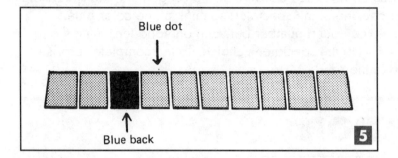

COMMENTS AND SUGGESTIONS

Carry the ten cards in their prearranged stack in a separate pocket so that you can remove the cards and place them on the table in a smooth, unhurried fashion. Practice placing the cards on the table until you can do it in a natural, relaxed manner. This effect can be presented either as a demonstration of ESP or as a magic trick. Never repeat this trick, or you will give away the principle used to force the special card.

CENTER TEAR

This is without doubt one of the simplest, yet cleverest, of all methods for learning the contents of a short message, a word, or a number written by a spectator. Properly performed, it is so deceptive that the spectators will have no idea trickery is involved, and many may be ready to accept it as a display of actual mind reading. Naturally, you should disclaim such power, but at the same time keep the secret to yourself, thus adding to a very perplexing mystery.

EFFECT

You give a spectator a square slip of paper and a pencil, telling the spectator to write a name, a number, or even a brief message in the center. This is done while your back is turned. Then the spectator folds the paper in half and then in quarters, so that you cannot possibly see the writing. You tear up the folded slip, drop the pieces into an ashtray, and burn them. You then reveal the spectator's message.

SECRET AND PREPARATION

A To prepare for this trick, you will need to place a pack of matches in your left pocket, and you will need to have an ashtray handy.

B Cut out a small slip of paper, approximately 3″ square. Draw a circle about 1¼″ wide in the center of one side of the paper, as shown.

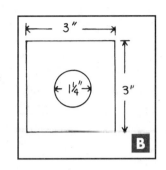

METHOD

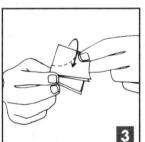

1 Give the paper to a spectator, and instruct the spectator to write a word or a short message within the "magic circle." Make sure that the person understands that you are not to see what is written on the paper.

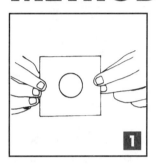

2 When the message is complete, instruct the spectator to fold the paper in half so that the writing is within the fold.

3 Have the person fold the paper once again, so it is folded in quarters.

4 Take the folded slip from the spectator. You can look at the packet and easily see which corner is actually the center, the magic circle, of the piece of paper.

NOTE: Practice folding the paper yourself. This will help you to instantly spot the desired corner.

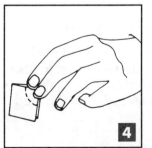

5 When you have located the center corner of the paper, hold the folded packet so that the magic circle is in the upper right-hand corner, facing you.

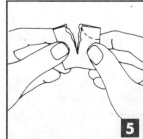

With the packet held in this manner, tear it in half. This tear should leave the magic circle undamaged.

6 Once you have torn the packet in half, place the left-hand pieces of paper behind the right-hand pieces. Hold all the pieces in your left hand. The magic circle should be at the top of the packet, and it should be nearest your body.

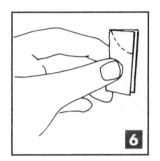

7 Rotate the packet a quarter turn to the right and grasp it between both hands. The magic circle is still facing you, held by your right thumb and first finger. Holding the packet in this position, tear it in half once more.

8 Place the left-hand pieces behind the right-hand pieces again. Take all the pieces in your right finger tips. The magic circle is still facing you and is right under your right thumb.

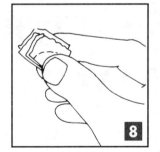

9 Hold all the pieces in your right hand, between your thumb and fingers. Position your right hand over the ashtray. Drop all of the pieces of paper—except the magic circle, which is held directly under your thumb—into the ashtray. As you release the pieces, use your thumb to slide the piece of paper containing the magic circle back toward the middle joints of your fingers.

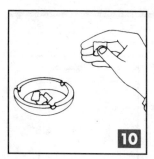

10 You hold the magic circle concealed in your right fingers. The rest of the pieces of paper have fallen into the ashtray. The spectators are unaware that you hold this paper (which contains the message) in your hand.

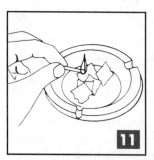

11 With the magic circle safely hidden in your right hand, use your left hand to reach into your pocket and take out the pack of matches. Use both hands to remove a match, strike it, and set fire to the pieces of paper in the ashtray. Place the pack of matches on the table with your right hand and use your left hand to hold the lighted match.

12 While the spectators are concentrating on the burning pieces of paper, drop your right hand below the table and use your right thumb to secretly open up the magic circle hidden in your right fingers. As soon as you have read the message, quietly crumple up or refold the paper. As the rest of the paper continues to burn, pick up the pack of matches and place them and the magic circle in your right pocket. Concentrate deeply on the rising smoke before you reveal the words of the message.

COMMENTS AND SUGGESTIONS

The most important thing to remember is that your right hand, while it secretly holds the center portion of the paper, must be held completely relaxed and natural. When you drop your right hand below the table to open up the paper and read the message, direct the spectators to focus their attention on the burning pieces of paper and the smoke as you glance at the message.

This is another classic method that is used not only by magicians, but also by fraudulent spirit mediums and psychics. Its great strength lies in that it uses only ordinary objects. With the proper buildup, this simple effect can be made into a real miracle!

CENTER TEAR— STANDING VARIATION

When working the CENTER TEAR away from a table, as you occasionally may have to do, you can use the following subterfuge.

METHOD

1 Light the match with your left hand, placing the pack in your right hand where it hides the torn center.

2 As you start to set fire to the pieces in the ashtray, place the pack of matches on the table.

3 Deliberately let the match go out while your right thumb is secretly opening the torn center.

4 Your right hand picks up the pack of matches in order to strike another match. Both hands are needed for that action, particularly if the left hand dawdles while lighting the pieces in the ashtray, giving you an opportunity to read the message.

5 Finally, the right hand can slide the pack of matches over the torn center, hiding it. You dispose of the torn center by simply dropping it in your right pocket along with the pack of matches.

SPECTRUM PREDICTION

Prediction effects form an important phase of mentalism and should be included on nearly every program. Moreover, where predictions are concerned, one good test definitely calls for another, because the more predictions you fulfill the less chance there is that luck has anything to do with it. Any good prediction may puzzle the spectators; but if you follow one with another, or even hit three in a row, people will really be bewildered. However, simply repeating the same prediction time after time is not the right policy. Some spectators lose interest when the same trick is repeated; others are apt to watch for a weak point and may be just sharp enough to spot it. So the answer is to have some special type of divination in reserve, differing from the rest in regard to objects used as well as method. The SPECTRUM PREDICTION meets both those qualifications.

EFFECT

You display eight brightly colored squares of cardboard and spread them out on the table so that everyone can see that each square or chip is a different color. You write a prediction on a piece of paper that you fold and give to a spectator to hold. The colored chips are gathered together by a spectator and wrapped in your opaque handkerchief. This same person is asked to reach into the folds of the handkerchief and withdraw a single chip. This done, the prediction is unfolded and read aloud. You are proved to be correct!

SECRET AND PREPARATION

A From a stationery or art supply store, obtain eight different colors of cardboard; or you may use colored construction paper, or even white cardboard that you have colored with paint, crayons, or ink. The colors you use are unimportant, but use easily recognizable colors such as yellow, blue, green, red, orange, purple, black, and white. In any event, make eight 1" squares, all of a different color. You also need to cut eight more squares that are all the same color. For the purpose of explanation, let's assume that these additional squares are all red. You therefore have eight different colored squares and eight squares that are all red.

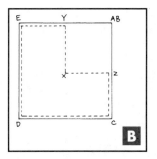

B You will also need two identical pocket handkerchiefs. Handkerchiefs made with a colored pattern work best. (Bandannas are good.) Place one on the other and sew them together, as shown by the dotted lines.

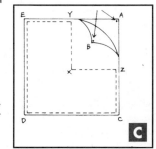

C You will notice that point X is the center of the handkerchief. The stitching along lines XY and XZ form a hidden pocket that can be opened at AB. Sew two small

beads at the A and B corners. These beads will enable you to find the pocket opening quickly. (The beads are optional, but they do help greatly in locating the secret pocket at the proper time.)

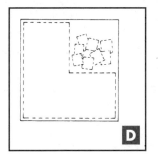

D Place the eight red squares in the hidden pocket. Grasp corners A and B and shake out the handkerchief. Place the prepared handkerchief in your coat pocket with corners A and B on top, where you can grasp them easily so that the extra, secret squares will not fall out when you remove the handkerchief.

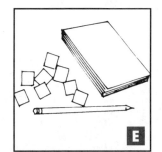

E Along with the eight squares of different colors, place a small pad of paper and a pencil on the table.

METHOD

1 Call the spectators' attention to the colored squares. Pick up the pad and, without letting the spectators see what you are writing, write, "You will select the color red." Tear the prediction from the pad and fold it so that it cannot be read by the spectators. Hand the folded slip to one of the spectators to hold.

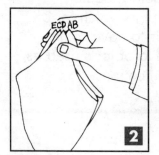

2 With your right hand, reach into your coat pocket and grasp the prepared handkerchief by the small beads that are sewn into the Corners A and B. Withdraw the handkerchief, show it on both sides, and gather all of the corners together, forming a bag, as shown.

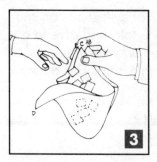

3 Have the spectator pick up the colored squares from the table. You are holding the hand-kerchief by the corners in your right hand. With your left thumb and first finger, release Corner D and allow the spectator to drop the squares into the handkerchief. These squares do not go into the secret pocket.

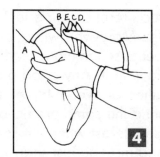

4 Shake the impromptu bag, mixing the colored squares inside. Release Corner A and allow the spectator to reach inside and remove a single square. The spectator will be reaching inside the hidden pocket that contains only red squares. Be sure the spectator removes only one of the squares.

5 Once the spectator has the red square, simply bunch up the handkerchief and put it back in your pocket, squares and all.

6 Ask the spectator to unfold the slip of paper. Again, you have proven your magical powers. Your prediction proves to be exactly correct!

COMMENTS AND SUGGESTIONS

The success of this trick depends upon handling the handkerchief in a natural, casual manner, so as to avoid suspicion. Since the handkerchief is a common article, it seems nothing more than a mere adjunct to the prediction. For that reason, it is comparatively easy to focus attention on the colored squares at the outset and the prediction slip at the finish, leaving the spectator with one red square and the prediction.

If you have an ordinary handkerchief resembling the special double handkerchief, you can use it in some previous effect in which it plays an innocent part. Place it in your pocket afterward. When you bring out the double handker-chief for the SPECTRUM PREDICTION, everyone will suppose it to be the same one that you used before. It is also a good plan to have eight extra squares of some color other than red, so that if you perform the prediction for the same group of people on another occasion, you can force a different color.

SPECTRUM PREDICTION—
NUMBER VARIATION

A clever and simple variation of the SPECTRUM PREDICTION is the use of the numbers one through eight, written on separate slips of paper, rather than the colored squares of cardboard used in the first version.

EFFECT

You display a pad of paper and openly write the numbers one through eight on individual sheets of paper from the pad. After all of the papers have been numbered, each is folded, first in half, and then in quarters. The entire lot is placed into a makeshift bag constructed from your handkerchief. You write an additional prediction number, which you do not let the spectators see, on one more slip of paper. This is folded and handed to one of the spectators to hold. A second spectator is asked to select one of the eight slips from the handkerchief. After the slip is selected, you open the handkerchief to show that only seven slips remain. The two spectators then open their papers. The slip containing the prediction is found to match exactly the "freely selected" number on the paper held by the second spectator.

SECRET AND PREPARATION

The secret of this trick is exactly the same as the SPECTRUM PREDICTION; however, it has certain advantages and one disadvantage. The disadvantage is that the colored slips in the first version are perhaps more spectacular and can certainly be seen from a greater distance if you are performing for a large group. The number variation, however, has the advantage of the "look" of a totally impromptu mystery because all of the props are ordinary objects, as opposed to the specially colored squares. Also, in the following method, the handkerchief may be opened so that the remaining slips fall out after the second spectator has made a selection.

Before the show, write the same number on eight slips of paper. Let's assume the number is five. Fold all of the slips and place them in the secret pocket of the double handkerchief just as you did in Step D of the SPECTRUM PREDICTION. Place the handkerchief in your pocket.

METHOD

1 Display a pad of paper (this must be the same paper as the previously written and folded slips) and openly write the numbers one through eight on different sheets from the pad. Write the number "1," tear that sheet off, fold it in half and into quarters, and place it on the table. Then write the number "2," tear it off, fold it, and place it on the table with the first. Continue until you have eight separate slips with different numbers.

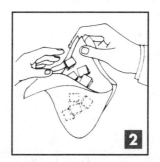

2 Just as you did in Step 2 of the SPECTRUM PREDICTION, remove the handkerchief from your pocket and, as in Step 3, form the handkerchief into a bag by holding it by the four corners. Place all eight slips in the main body of the handkerchief. Do not put the slips in the secret pocket.

3 Ask the spectator to reach into the handkerchief and remove one of the slips. The spectator should hold the slip tightly so that no one can see what number is written on it until the conclusion of the effect. As you explain this to the spectator, you demonstrate the actions at the same time. Reach into the bag (be sure you reach into the main body of the handkerchief, not the secret compartment) and remove one of the regular slips. After explaining that the spectator is to hold the slip tightly, put your hand back into the handkerchief, apparently replacing the slip. Really, you secretly hold the slip in your palm and remove your hand as if it were empty.

NOTE: You will find this quite easy to do as the spectators are not expecting trickery of any kind at this point.

4 Reach into your pocket and remove the pencil. At the same time, leave the extra slip, which you have just palmed, in your pocket. Gaze intently at the spectator who will select the slip, as if to gain a mental impression of their future actions. Then pick up the pad with your other hand and write the prediction (the number five) on the pad. Tear off the slip, fold it, and hand it to some other spectator to hold.

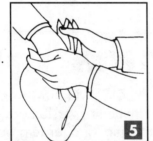

5 Ask the first spectator to reach into the handkerchief and

remove one of the slips. Be sure that you open the handkerchief, as you did in Step 4 of the SPECTRUM PREDICTION, so that the spectator will remove one of the force papers.

6 Open up the handkerchief, holding Corners A and B gathered in your right hand (so that the secret force slips do not fall out), and let the seven remaining slips in the main portion of the handkerchief fall on the table.

7 Place the handkerchief in your pocket (along with the force slips). With your right hand, pick the slips up one at a time and count them, without unfolding them, from the table into your left hand. Indicate that the spectator had a free selection of any of the eight slips, as you openly place the seven pieces of paper in your pocket.

8 Have the second spectator open the prediction slip and read the number aloud. Emphasize again the free selection that the first spectator had. Have the first spectator open the slip for the first time and read the freely selected number. The two numbers match! You have just presented what appears to be another completely impromptu mental miracle.

PING-PONG PRESTIDIGITATION

Here is a comedy trick in which you let everyone in on the secret of the effect except for one person—the spectator who assists you on stage. This is the only person who is deceived by your magical methods, creating a situation that develops into good fun for everyone.

EFFECT

You display three pairs of different colored ping-pong balls. One pair is white, one pair is red, and one pair is blue. You drop all six balls into a paper bag and invite two spectators to assist in the effect. The spectator on your left is asked to reach in the bag—without looking—and remove any ball. No matter which ball is withdrawn, the other spectator is able to reach into the bag and remove the matching ball without looking inside the bag. The selected balls are replaced, and the trick is repeated over and over again with the same improbable results.

SECRET AND PREPARATION

What the first spectator doesn't know is that everyone else, including the other spectator, can see the colored balls all along through a secret "window" in the side of the bag! Because of the secret window, everyone sees how the trick works, except for the spectator on the left who is unaware throughout the presentation that the bag is cleverly gimmicked.

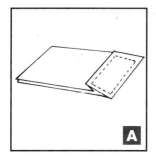

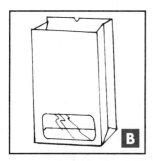

A To prepare, obtain an ordinary brown paper bag, about the size of a standard lunch bag. Cut a hole in the side of the bag, as shown. The position of the hole should be such that it is completely hidden from view by the bottom portion of the bag when the bag is folded flat. This way, the bag can be freely shown on both sides and handled quite casually before it is opened to begin the effect.

B Glue or tape a piece of transparent kitchen wrap (clear plastic) over the hole so that the balls will not fall out of the bag during the presentation. The

construction of the bag is complete. As you can see, a sort of window has been formed in the bag, allowing you to see into the bag quite easily.

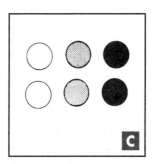

C Purchase six ordinary ping-pong balls. Prepare the three pairs of balls by painting or coloring them in three brightly contrasting colors. Permanent-ink marking pens also work well for coloring the balls and can be purchased at most stationery stores. Instead of ping-pong balls, you can use lightweight plastic or rubber balls. These can be obtained at department or toy stores. Be sure they are all the same size and are made of the same material, so that it is impossible to distinguish one color from another without looking at them.

METHOD

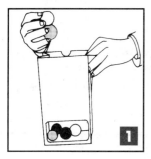

1 Invite two spectators to help you. Position yourself between them, facing the audience. Display the balls and call attention to the fact that there are three pairs of different colored balls. Pick up the bag and display it—folded flat—so that everyone (especially the spectator on the left) can see that it is quite ordinary. Open the bag so that the window faces the audience (and not the spectator on your left) and openly drop the six balls into the bag. The audience will immediately see that the bag is gimmicked. They will begin to see why, as you continue.

2 Ask the spectator on your left to reach into the bag—without looking—and remove one ball. Tell the spectator to keep it concealed, so that no one else knows its color. Be sure to hold the bag so that the window is facing away from this person, who must not see that the bag is prepared.

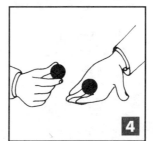

3 After the spectator removes the ball, swing your body to the right and ask the other spectator to concentrate very hard, to reach into the bag, and to try to remove the matching colored ball. Be sure to hold the bag so that the window faces this person, who of course will catch on immediately. It is a simple matter for the spectator to remove the correct ball, as it will be the only ball inside the bag without a matching color.

4 Once the second spectator has removed the ball, have both openly display the two selected balls to the audience. Since the spectator on your right has removed the correct ball, the two balls will match in color.

5 Have both spectators replace the balls in the bag and perform the effect a few more times. Each time the trick is successful, the reaction of the spectator on your left will become more and more humorous. Because this person is unaware of the secret window, there will be no way to explain this seemingly impossible series of coincidences.

COMMENTS AND SUGGESTIONS

At the end of the trick, you should humorously reveal the secret to the puzzled spectator by "accidentally" turning the window side of the bag toward that person as you reach out to shake hands. Thank both of the spectators for being such good sports as they rejoin the audience.

This is a good trick to work at a party, when you are waiting for more people to arrive before you begin your regular show. After the spectator on the left has been utterly baffled, you suggest that next time, they can play the part of the spectator on the right. When some newcomers arrive, you repeat the trick, inviting one of them to serve as the spectator on your left. Your former victim, now the spectator on your right, has the pleasure of seeing how nicely the trick works. This procedure can be repeated with other new arrivals, making an excellent prelude for your show.

NOTE: You must be careful, in presenting tricks of this nature, that you don't offend or insult the intelligence of the spectator who is unaware of the working of the effect. Present the trick in a warm, humorous style so that the spectator does not get annoyed.

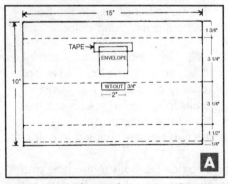

ENVELOPE STAND

With mental tests, it is a good idea to use props only if they make the presentation more direct and more effective. When such devices actually aid in the deception, without the spectators realizing it, the effect is even better. This is especially true of the ENVELOPE STAND.

EFFECT

You display an attractive pasteboard stand with five numbered envelopes arranged on it. You announce that one of the sealed envelopes contains a dollar bill and the rest are empty. A spectator is given a free choice of any envelope. When the chosen envelope is opened, it is found to contain the dollar bill. It appears as if you have been able to influence the decision of the spectator.

SECRET AND PREPARATION

A Actually, all five envelopes are empty. The stand is constructed in such a way as to deliver the bill into any selected envelope. Construct the stand as shown. Use a piece of cardboard about 10" x 15" (depending upon the size of the envelopes). Cut out a hole in the center of the back of the stand. Tape the lower portion of an envelope that you have cut in half to the back of the cardboard just below the opening.

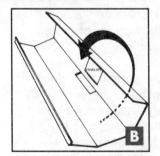

B Fold the cardboard as shown by the dotted lines so that the half-envelope is hidden inside the triangular body of the stand.

C This illustration shows the completed stand. Notice the turned up "lip" located on the front edge of the stand. This ledge prevents the envelopes from slipping off the stand.

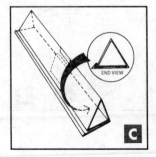

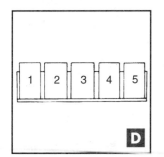

D Arrange five numbered envelopes on the face of the stand. Secretly place a folded dollar bill out of sight in the half-envelope.

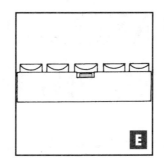

E This is a view from the rear. Notice how the dollar bill protrudes slightly from the hole behind the center envelope. The top edge of the bill extends ¼" or so from the hole and cannot be seen from the front side of the stand.

METHOD

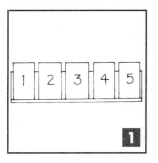

1 To perform the trick, display the stand and call attention to the five numbered envelopes displayed on the stand. (Small coin or pay envelopes work best.) Announce that before the trick, you placed a dollar bill in only one of the envelopes. Predict that the envelope with the dollar will be chosen at random by a spectator. Select a spectator. Allow this person to choose any envelope. Give the spectator the opportunity to change their choice.

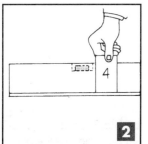

2 Remove all envelopes not chosen from the stand.

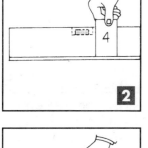

3 Place the selected envelope, in this case Number 4, directly in front of the secret hole in the stand.

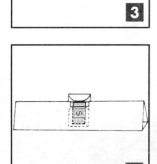

4 Here is the rear view of the stand at this point in the routine. Notice how the bill in the half-envelope protrudes slightly from the hole in the stand.

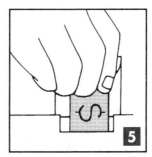

5 Remove the selected envelope from the stand with the thumb and fingers of your right hand and, as you do, secretly grasp the upper end of the hidden bill with your right fingers. Hold the dollar bill firmly behind the selected envelope as you remove the envelope from the stand. Be sure not to expose the bill hidden behind it.

6 Casually transfer the envelope (and the hidden bill) to your left hand. The left thumb holds the bill against the back of the envelope. This move gives the spectators a chance to see that both of your hands are empty. With your free right hand, tear off one end of the sealed envelope. Be sure not to prematurely expose the bill.

7 Insert your right first and second fingers into the envelope and appear to remove the bill from inside. Actually, you pull the bill out from behind the envelope using your right thumb. Display the folded bill, hold between the thumb and fingers of your right hand.

8 Unfold the bill and show it to be authentic before you pick up the other four envelopes. Tear these envelopes in half to show that they are all empty—or better yet, have the audience open and examine them. You may reward your spectator with the dollar as a souvenir if you wish. In any event, hand the remains of all of the envelopes to your audience for inspection.

ENVELOPE STAND— BANK NIGHT VARIATION

EFFECT

A comedy variation of this mystery can be worked with four spectators. The spectators are informed that only one of the envelopes contains a real bill—the rest have only blank slips of paper. Each spectator will be allowed to choose any envelope. You state that whoever picks the envelope with the dollar bill can keep it. You explain that you will keep only the final envelope for yourself. Thus the spectators do all of the choosing. When the spectators open their envelopes, they find blank pieces of paper that are the size of a dollar bill. You then open your envelope and remove the real dollar bill!

SECRET AND PREPARATION

The trick works exactly the same as the ENVELOPE STAND, except that you must be sure that all the envelopes are opaque since the spectators will have an opportunity to handle them and change their minds. Therefore the possibility exists that they could see through an envelope made of lightweight paper.

Cut five blank pieces of paper the same size as a dollar bill and place one in each of the five numbered envelopes. Conceal the dollar bill in the envelope stand as before.

METHOD

1 Explain that only one envelope contains a dollar bill and that the lucky spectator who selects it will get to keep it.

2 Have each spectator call out the number of the envelope that person wants. When each choice is made, you hand the envelope to the spectator. In this way, the spectators never have a chance to come near the stand and discover its secret.

3 After each spectator has an envelope, position the remaining envelope in the center of the stand—directly in front of the hidden bill.

4 Emphasize the fairness of the selection and then have all of the spectators open their envelopes, one at a time. The suspense builds, and the odds grow shorter, as the contents of each envelope are revealed.

5 Just as the last spectator removes the blank paper, pick up your envelope and steal the bill from the stand. All eyes will be on the spectator at this time, which will aid in the misdirection as you remove the remaining envelope and the bill.

6 Open your envelope and remove (from behind) the real dollar.

7 Thank the spectators as you crumple up your envelope (with the last blank paper inside). Casually place the envelope on the table as you display the dollar to the spectators!

THREE-WAY TEST

Reading a person's mind is surely a most effective way of demonstrating your magical powers. In this ESP experiment, you show your ability to predict and control the minds of three spectators. This effect requires a little closer study than most magic tricks, but it is well worth the sensational impact of your magical mind reading.

EFFECT

A In this mental effect, you demonstrate three different experiments in extrasensory perception. In the first experiment, you correctly determine the exact amount of change in a spectator's pockets.

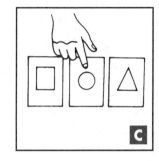

C In the last experiment, you correctly predict which of three figure drawings a spectator will select from the table. With a small pad and pencil on your table, you are ready to begin.

B In the second test, you receive a mental impression of an object that a spectator is thinking of before the spectator picks it up.

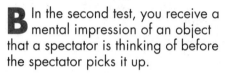

METHOD

First, explain that you are going to demonstrate three different forms of ESP. To do this, you need three spectators to assist you, one person for each test. Continue by asking the members of the audience to assemble four or more small objects from around the room and to place them on the table in front of one of the spectators.

1 These can be any objects, as long as they are all different. Let's assume that the four items gathered are an ashtray, a pen, a matchbook, and a paper clip.

2 Pick up a pad of paper and tear off three of the blank sheets. On one sheet of paper, draw a circle; on the second, draw a square; and on the third, draw a triangle. Place these slips face up in a row in front of one of the spectators.

3 Say to another one of the spectators, "Reach into your pocket or purse and bring out all of the small change you have there." Tell the spectator not to

count it but to keep it held tightly in a closed fist.

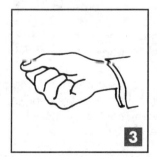

4 You are now ready to begin the actual experiments. Explain that the first experiment is a test of clairvoyance, which is the ability to see hidden objects.

5 Pick up the pad and pencil and hold it so no one can see what you write. To the "money" spectator, say, "I am now going to write down my impression of the amount of change in your hand." Obviously, you can't write this amount, because you don't know it yet! Instead, draw a circle on the slip of paper.

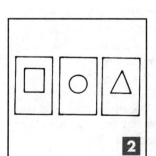

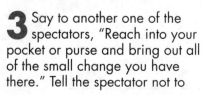

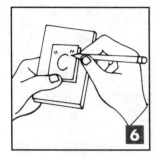

6 Tear off the slip and fold it without letting anyone see what you have written. Say that you will call this first test "Test A" and that you will write the letter "A" on the outside of the slip. Instead, you really mark it with the letter "C."

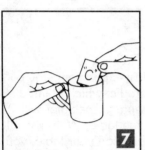

7 After you have marked the slip, place it where it will be out of view of the spectators. (Be careful not to let anyone see the letter "C" on the slip of paper.) A drinking glass or a coffee cup works well if it is the type you can't see through.

8 Another suggestion would be to turn an ashtray or saucer upside down on the table and place the slip under it. It's not important where you place the slip as long as the letter written on the outside cannot be seen by the spectators. Let's assume you place the slip in a coffee mug.

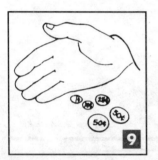

9 After the folded slip is in the mug, tell Person A to count the money out onto the table and leave it there for everyone to see. Let's say it comes to exactly $1.36.

10 You turn to the second person and say, "I'm going to try a test in telepathy with you. This means that I can mentally pick up an impression that you already have in your mind. To do this, I want you to concentrate on one of the four objects on the table, the object you are going to pick up in your hand. Tell me when you have decided on the one you want, but don't tell me which object, and don't pick it up until after I have written down my impression."

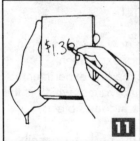

11 Instead of writing on the pad the name of one of the objects (because you don't know which one the spectator is thinking of), you write the amount of change that has been counted on the table from Test A, $1.36.

NOTE: Learning information from one test and secretly using it in the next test is called the One-Ahead Principle.

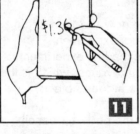

12 Tear off this sheet and fold it. Tell the spectator that this is Test B and you will mark the slip with the letter "B." But, instead of writing "B," you mark it with the letter "A."

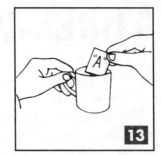

13 Put this slip into the mug along with the other one.

14 Tell the spectator who was concentrating on an object to pick it up. Let's say this spectator picks up the matchbook.

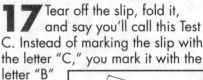

15 Tell the third spectator that you will do an experiment in precognition. This means that you will predict a certain result before the spectator decides to do it.

16 Pretend to write a prediction on the pad, but really write down the object in Person B's hand, the matchbook.

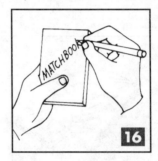

17 Tear off the slip, fold it, and say you'll call this Test C. Instead of marking the slip with the letter "C," you mark it with the letter "B" as shown.

18 Place this slip into the mug along with the other two.

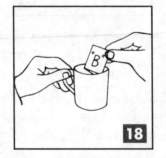

19 You must maneuver the spectator into selecting the slip of paper with the circle on it. This is called "Forcing," although the spectator believes it is a free choice. The force you will use here is called the MAGICIAN'S CHOICE FORCE (see page 9).

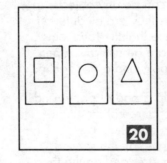

20 Point out to the spectator that you have drawn a different figure on each of the three papers on the table. Ask the spectator to point to any one of the three slips. One of several situations will arise.

21 First situation: If they point to the circle, say, "Please pick up the slip that you have selected and hold it in your hand."

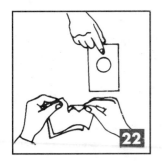

22 When the spectator does this, you pick up the other two slips and tear them up, saying, "We will not need these, so I'll tear them up."

23 Second situation: If the spectator points to the square or the triangle, you pick up the one the spectator pointed to.

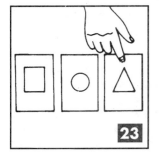

24 After picking up the spectator's choice, you say, "Fine, I'll tear this one up and that leaves only two."

25 Ask your spectator to pick up either one of the remaining slips of paper. Either one of two things will now happen.

26 The spectator may pick up the paper with the circle on it.

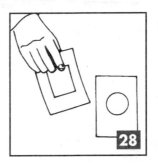

27 If that happens, then you pick up the one remaining slip on the table and tear it up, saying, "OK, the circle is the one you selected, so we won't need this one either."

28 The spectator may pick up the paper without the circle on it.

29 If that happens, you say, "OK, you tear up that slip, which leaves just the one on the table." Of course, the one that is left is the circle.

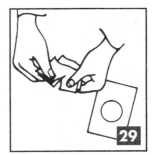

30 Once you have successfully "forced" the circle, you are ready for the payoff. Pick up the mug and dump the slips onto the table. Ask each spectator to take the slip that has the appropriate letter on it, and open it. When each slip is opened, all three of your tests prove to be correct!

COMMENTS AND SUGGESTIONS

This is a very strong trick. It can be performed anywhere. All you need are a pencil and some pieces of paper. There is no sleight of hand or special skill needed. However, it is a trick that must be studied thoroughly and practiced until you can remember easily which part comes next, which letter to write on each slip, etc. After you have mastered it, you will be able to baffle your friends with one of the finest "mind reading" mysteries in the entire Art of Magic.

MAGAZINE TEST

Among mental mysteries, those in which a spectator does all the work can be rated among the best, for this apparently makes it impossible for the performer to inject any element of trickery. In fact, there are tricks in which the magician does nothing more than guide the spectator's actions. The MAGAZINE TEST is one such trick. You will find, however, that it does involve a small bit of work on your part, but this is mostly done beforehand. Hence, no one even knows about it, making the trick all the more effective.

EFFECT

Displaying a sealed envelope and a current issue of a well-known magazine, you explain to the audience that, prior to your appearance, you wrote one word on a white card and sealed it in an envelope. This envelope you now hand to one of the spectators in the audience. Ask a second spectator to join you on stage in order to demonstrate your ability to "see into the future." You hand the magazine to the second spectator along with a pencil or felt-tipped pen. In order not to influence the spectator's choice of a word from the magazine, ask this spectator to hold the magazine behind their back and to mark a page at random with a bold X. After you take back the now-closed magazine you ask the first spectator to tear open the envelope you gave them at the start and to read the predicted word. When the magazine is opened to the marked page, the audience is surprised to see that the intersecting lines of the X are directly through the identical word.

SECRET AND PREPARATION

A Select a current issue of a magazine. Turn to any right-hand page located near the center of the magazine and draw a large X on the page. Make the mark so that the two lines of the X cross over a single word, as shown. From this point on, this word, "news," will be referred to as the force word.

NOTE: You should try marking the magazine page behind your own back before trying this trick. In fact, several trials are advisable in order to see just what a pair of crossed lines will look like when a spectator goes through the same procedure. Then, when you are ready to prepare the magazine that you intend to use in the test, you can copy one of your previous attempts, giving the lines slight curves or an irregular appearance to make them look authentic. Never

have them cross exactly in the center of the forced word. Hit near one end, or just above or below, yet close enough so everyone will agree on that word.

B Print the force word across the face of a white card and seal the "prediction" in an opaque envelope.

C The final step is to prepare a pen or pencil to prevent the spectator from actually making a mark on the magazine. Be sure that this pen or pencil matches the one you used to mark the page. The best pen to use is a felt-tip one. Let it sit without the cap on until the tip is dried out. A ballpoint pen, which is out of ink, also works well. If a pencil is used, dip the tip in clear varnish and allow it to dry overnight. This will prevent the pencil from making a mark.

METHOD

1 Display the sealed envelope with the force word written on the card inside. Have a member of the audience hold the envelope. Pick up the magazine and demonstrate for the audience how you would like a spectator to mark the magazine page. Tell the spectator to face the audience and thumb through the magazine while holding it behind their back. Once the spectator has selected a page, demonstrate how to fold the left-hand pages of the magazine to the rear. This ensures that the spectator will mark on a right-hand page of the magazine.

2 When you are sure that the spectator understands the proper procedure for marking the magazine, supply the prepared pen or pencil. Have the spectator hold the magazine behind their back, select any (right-hand) page, fold the other (left-hand) pages out of the way, and mark the page with a large X. The prepared pen or pencil will ensure that no mark is actually made.

3 Have the spectator close the magazine before bringing it out from behind their back. Take the pen or pencil and the magazine from the spectator. Put the pen or pencil away in your pocket as soon as you have finished this phase of the trick.

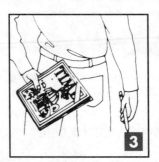

4 Call attention to the sealed envelope that is being held by a member of the audience. Emphasize that the envelope was given to the spectator before the magazine was marked. Have the person holding the envelope tear it open and call out the word written on the card inside.

5 Give the magazine back to the spectator who marked the page and have them look through the pages until the marked page is located. When it is found, have the spectator call out the word that is indicated by that mark. It will match the force word that was written on the prediction card!

CHAPTER 4
CUP-AND-BALL
TRICKS

Unquestionably, CUPS AND BALLS is one of the oldest routines in the Art of Magic. Historians tell us it was first performed in antiquity by jugglers who embellished their usual juggling routines with sleight of hand. The most common trick was to put a pebble under one cup and have it disappear, only to be found beneath another cup. This sleight of hand was practiced by the ancient Egyptians and later by the Greeks and Romans.

In the Middle Ages, jesters and minstrels performed their share of magic along with jugglers, and in many instances, CUPS AND BALLS had become their mainstay. Numerous prints from around the year 1500 show performers at tables manipulating conical-shaped cups with small balls of cork—a great improvement over the pebbles used in ancient times. The trick was so successful that it remained virtually unchanged during the next 400 years.

Since the Middle Ages, however, the routine has been simplified and modernized to suit the needs of today's close-up magicians. So the descriptions that appear in the following section may prove amazing even to our predecessors!

FINGER-PALM VANISH

EFFECT

In this vanish, a coin, ball, or other small object is actually retained in the same spot in your left hand from start to finish. You will need to learn this vanish before practicing CUPS AND BALLS and SPONGE SORCERY in this book. The instruction is given with two sets of illustrations. Those at the left show how it appears to you, the performer; those at the right represent the spectators' view.

METHOD

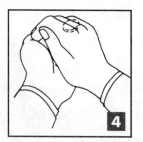

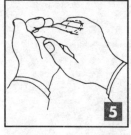

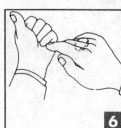

1 Display a coin lying on the fingers of your right hand, as shown.

2 Your left hand is held palm up, about waist high, with your left fingers pointing just to the right of the center of where the spectators are sitting or gathered. The little finger of your right hand rests across the tips of your left fingers.

3 Turn your right hand over toward you. At the same time, curl your right fingers inward just enough to hold the coin securely in the right fingers, as shown. The coin is now in the finger-palm position.

4 Tip your right hand over even more. This is the moment when the coin should be falling into your left hand. Actually, the right hand secretly retains the coin in the finger-palm position.

5 Your left fingers close, as if they contained the coin. Your right hand begins to move away from your left hand, with the coin secretly finger-palmed.

6 As your left hand closes into a loose fist, your right hand pauses briefly, pointing the first finger toward the closed left hand, attracting attention to the left hand.

7 Lower your right hand casually to your side as your eyes follow your left hand. This is misdirection.

8 The left hand is now on its own. It apparently squeezes the coin into nothing and opens to show that the coin has vanished.

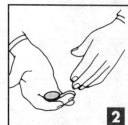

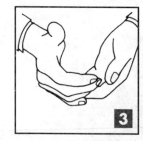
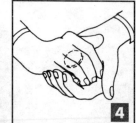

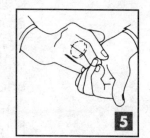

CUPS AND BALLS

This classic of magic deserves a top rating, for although it dates back to ancient times, it has maintained its popularity throughout the centuries. Even though it is among the oldest of magical effects, it always seems new. The following routine gives the appearance of requiring great skill, yet actually the basic moves are comparatively simple. This is because CUPS AND BALLS combines misdirection with the element of surprise so that the spectators never know what to expect next.

EFFECT

On the table before you are three empty cups and three small colored balls. You position the three balls in a horizontal row and place a cup, mouth down, behind each ball. You place one of the balls on top of the center cup and stack the remaining two cups on top of the first, imprisoning the ball between them. Upon lifting the stack of cups as a group, the ball is found to have mysteriously penetrated through the center cup and now rests on the table. This baffling process is repeated with the two remaining balls until all three balls have magically gathered beneath the stack of cups. Then you vary your procedure by causing a single ball to vanish from your hand and appear beneath the center cup on the table.

Next, you place a ball beneath each cup. You then mysteriously cause the ball under the center cup to vanish and join the ball under the right-hand cup. From there, it vanishes once again and reappears with the ball under the left-hand cup. You place the three balls in your pocket, one at a time, only to find that they have once again appeared beneath the cups on the table. This procedure is repeated once more, when suddenly you reveal the surprise appearance of three full-size lemons, one beneath each cup.

SECRET AND PREPARATION

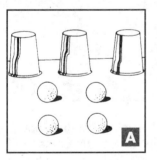

A You will need to acquire the proper type of cups in order to perform this routine effectively. The cups should nest within each other easily and leave enough space between each cup to permit the concealment of a ball between them. (See Comments and Suggestions.) You will also need four small identical balls of the appropriate size to be used with the cups. The only other props you will need are three ordinary lemons, or three small potatoes, or three small rubber balls. The primary requirement for these props is that each can fit easily inside one of the cups.

B To set up the apparatus for the start of the routine, place one of the cups mouth down on your table and put a ball on top of it. Nest the other two cups on the first, concealing the ball between the first and second cups.

C Turn the entire stack mouth up and drop the three remaining balls into the top cup of the stack. Throughout the presentation, the spectators should only be aware of three balls. The primary secret of the entire routine is the hidden fourth ball.

D At the start, have the three lemons in your right pocket. The lemons are not used until the final phase of the routine, but it is a good idea to practice with them in position so that you become used to their presence as you practice.

NOTE: To make CUPS AND BALLS easy to learn, the routine has been broken down into separate phases. Learn each phase before proceeding to the next. Practice the entire routine from start to finish, until each portion becomes smooth and natural.

METHOD
PHASE 1—PENETRATION

All of the illustrations in this phase are from the spectators' viewpoint.

1 Stand at the table with the spectators across from you. Pick up the cups with your left hand and tip the three balls from the top cup of the stack onto the table. With your right hand, arrange the balls in a horizontal row. The stack of nested cups is held in your left hand so that the bottom of the cups slants toward the table and the mouth of the cups tilts slightly up toward you, as shown. This angle is important in order to prevent the spectators from seeing into the cups during the performance of the following steps.

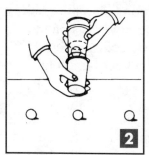

2 With your right hand, draw the bottom cup from the stack downward, as shown.

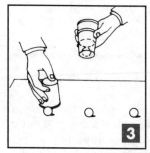

3 In one continuous flowing motion, turn the cup, mouth down, and place it on the table behind the ball at the right end of the row.

4 Remove the second cup from the stack in the same manner.

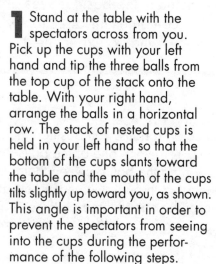

5 Place the second cup, mouth down, on the table behind the center ball.

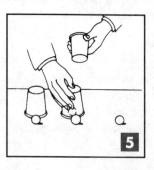

NOTE: You can now see why the cups must be tilted slightly toward you since this cup is concealing the fourth ball. If this step is executed in a smooth, unbroken motion, the fourth ball will be carried along inside the cup to the table, unnoticed by the spectators.

6 Grasp the last cup in your hand.

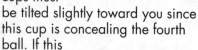

7 Place the last cup, mouth down, behind the ball at the left end of the row.

NOTE: It is important that the placement of the individual cups on the table be executed at the same exact pace so as not to attract attention to the center cup.

8 The three cups, mouth down, are now on the table, with the extra ball secretly under the center cup. The three visible balls are positioned in front of the cups, as shown.

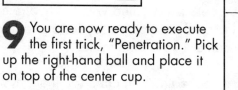

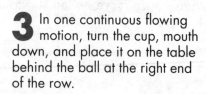

9 You are now ready to execute the first trick, "Penetration." Pick up the right-hand ball and place it on top of the center cup.

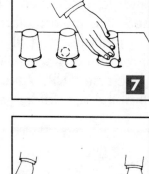

10 Lift the right-hand cup and nest it over the center cup, imprisoning the ball between the two cups, as shown.

11 Pick up the left-hand cup and add it to the stack.

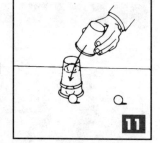

12 With your right first finger, tap the top cup of the stack and say, "I'll make the first ball penetrate the cup."

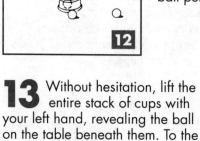

13 Without hesitation, lift the entire stack of cups with your left hand, revealing the ball on the table beneath them. To the spectators, it will look as if the ball you placed on the center cup penetrated the solid bottom of the cup and landed on the table!

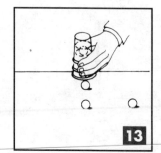

14 Holding the three cups together in your left hand, turn your left palm up so that the cups are positioned just as they were in Step 1.

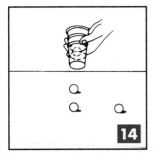

15 Repeat the same series of moves that you used in Steps 2 through 7. Remove the bottom cup and place it, mouth down, on the table to your right. Remove the second cup (which now contains the secret ball) and set it, mouth down, over the ball that just penetrated the cup in the previous sequence. Unknown to the spectators, there are now two balls under this cup, instead of one. Place the last cup, mouth down, behind the left-hand ball. The

situation should be as shown here.

16 You are now ready to execute the second penetration. Pick up the ball in front of the center cup and place it on top of the center cup.

17 Nest the other two cups, one at a time, over the center cup and the ball, just as you did in Steps 10 and 11.

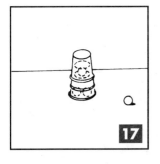

18 Tap the top cup once with your right finger and say, "Now I'll make the second ball penetrate the cup."

19 Immediately lift the stack of three cups, revealing the two balls beneath them. To the spectators, it appears as if the ball on the second cup penetrated through the cup to join the other ball beneath it.

20 Once again, turn your left palm up, holding the cups in the basic starting position as in Step 1.

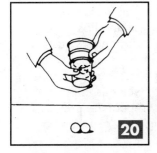

21 Repeat the same sequence again (Steps 2 through 7), placing the cups, one at a time, mouth down on the table. Be sure to place the second cup containing the secret ball over the two balls, which have already penetrated through the cup.

22 Repeat the same series of moves (Steps 8 through 13) to penetrate the last ball. Pick up the ball and place it on top of the center cup.

23 Nest the other two cups over the ball and tap the top cup to make the ball magically penetrate the cup.

24 Lift the stack to reveal all three balls on the table, beneath the center cup.

NOTE: Before continuing, be sure you have mastered the first phase of the routine. When you can perform it smoothly and with confidence from start to finish, you are ready to move on to the second phase.

PHASE 2— INVISIBLE FLIGHT

All of the illustrations in Phase 2 are from the spectators' viewpoint.

25 While holding the stack of cups in your left hand in the basic starting position, arrange the three balls on the table in a horizontal row before you. Place the three cups, one at a time, mouth down, behind the three balls, as shown here. The secret ball will once again be carried along, unnoticed, inside the center cup to the table.

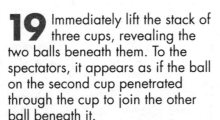

26 With your right hand, pick up the ball in front of the center cup and display it briefly on your right fingers in readiness for the FINGER-PALM VANISH (see page 70).

27 Apparently transfer the ball to your left hand using the FINGER-PALM VANISH. The spectators will believe that you have merely placed the ball into your left hand. Actually, the ball is secretly retained in the fingers of your right hand.

28 Casually lower your right hand and make a tossing motion with your left hand, as if to throw the ball invisibly from your left fist into the center cup.

29 With your left hand, lift the center cup and roll the ball slightly forward to reveal its magical arrival.

30 Set the center cup on the table, mouth down, behind the center ball. This is a very important phase of the routine, as it allows you to get the secret ball out of the cups and into your hand where you can use it to execute the next series of impossibilities described in Phase 3.

31 Still holding the secret ball in the finger-palm position in your right hand, pick up the ball in front of the cup on the right with the tips of your right thumb and fingers, as shown.

PHASE 3— ANY CUP CALLED FOR

The illustrations are from the spectators' and from your viewpoint, as indicated.

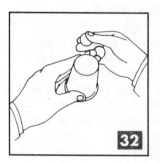

32 Here is a view of this action from your point of view. Notice how the visible ball is held between the thumb and first finger, while the secret ball is still concealed in the curled fingers. As you pick up the ball, your left hand grasps the right cup near the mouth, as shown.

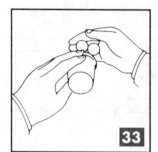

33 Tilt the cup back toward you, leaving the rear edge of the cup resting on the table. At the same time, allow the visible ball to roll alongside the secret ball in your curled fingers.

34 Without hesitation, slip both balls well under the front edge of the cup, as shown.

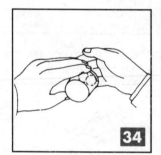

35 Here is a view of this action from the spectators' point of view. The spectators will believe that you are placing only one ball under the cup.

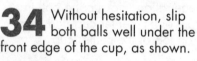

36 As you hold the balls under the cup, tilt the cup down and withdraw your fingers, leaving both balls beneath the cup.

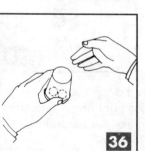

37 Without pausing, pick up the ball in front of the center cup with the tips of your right thumb and fingers, just as you did with the first ball in Step 31. At the same time grasp the center cup, which is in position to apparently repeat the previous series of moves—as when you placed the ball(s) under the right cup.

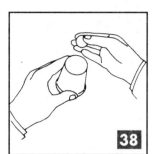

38 Here is the situation as seen from your point of view. Notice how the ball is held against the second and third fingers with your thumb.

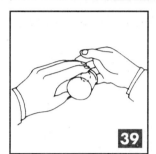

39 Tip the center cup back on its edge and move your right fingers and the ball under the front edge of the cup, as shown.

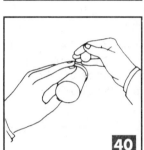

40 As soon as your fingers are well beneath the cup, remove your thumb from the ball and hold the ball with your right fingers, as shown. Withdraw your hand, secretly carrying the ball along. As you withdraw your hand from beneath the cup, be sure to tilt the back of your hand toward the spectators, so no one will see that you still hold the ball in your fingers instead of leaving it under the cup.

41 Immediately lower the front edge of the cup to the table as you remove your fingers and the ball from beneath the cup. The spectators believe that you merely placed the second ball under the center cup.

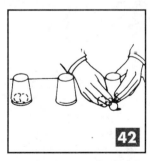

42 Without hesitation, move your right hand (still concealing the ball) to the last visible ball. Pick this up with your right thumb and fingers (just as you did in Step 31), as your left hand grasps the cup.

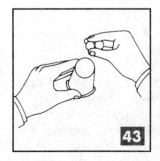

43 You are now going to repeat Steps 32 through 36 with the third cup. With your left hand, tip the third cup back on its edge and place both balls under the cup, "as one," as shown in this illustration from your point of view.

44 Here is the same action as seen from the spectators' point of view. To the spectators, it should appear as if you are merely placing a single ball under the third cup, just as you did with the other cups.

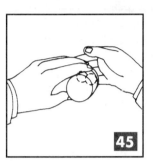

45 Lower the front edge of the cup, allowing it to drag both balls from your fingers as you withdraw your hand.

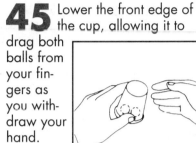
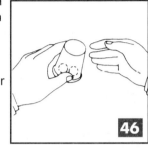

46 As soon as your fingers clear the front edge of the cup, set the mouth of the cup down, flush with the top of the table.

47 At this point, the spectators believe that you have simply placed one ball under each of the three cups. Actually, as the illustration shows, you have two balls under both end cups and nothing under the center cup.

48 State that you will cause the ball under the center cup to vanish and appear beneath whichever end cup the spectator wishes. Assuming the spectator chooses the right-hand cup, slowly tip over the center cup, allowing your spectators to see that the ball you placed under that cup has vanished. Leave the center cup on its side on the table, as shown.

49 Tip over the selected cup (in this case, the right-hand cup) to reveal the mysterious arrival of the missing ball, apparently joining the ball already under that cup.

50 With your right hand, pick up one of the two balls and display it at the base of your curled fingers in readiness for the FINGER-PALM VANISH. As you display the ball, make some comment about how difficult it is to keep track of that particular ball.

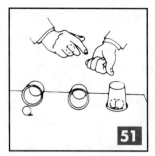

51 With that, apparently transfer the ball into your left hand, executing the FINGER-PALM VANISH. Actually, the ball is secretly retained in your right fingers, as shown.

52 Your left hand (which the spectators believe contains the ball) makes a tossing motion toward the left cup. As you "toss" the ball, open your left hand and show that the ball has vanished. At the same time, your right hand drops casually to your right side, carrying the secret ball with it.

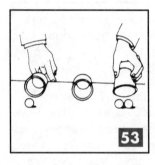

53 With your empty left hand, tip the left cup over and reveal the missing ball to complete the sequence.

NOTE: After mastering this phase, combine the first three phases into a smooth routine. When you have accomplished this and feel confident of all of the moves, you will be ready to learn Phase 4.

PHASE 4 — REPEAT PRODUCTION

All of the illustrations in Phase 4 are from the spectators' viewpoint.

54 After the conclusion of Phase 3, rearrange the three visible balls in a horizontal row and place one cup, mouth down, over each ball, as shown. The secret ball is still concealed in the curled fingers of your right hand.

55 With your left hand, lift the cup on the right.

56 Without pausing, turn the cup mouth up and transfer it to your right hand, which contains the secret ball.

57 Without hesitation, pick up the ball that was under the cup with your left fingers. At the same time, release your grip on the palmed ball in your right hand and allow it to secretly roll into the cup, as shown.

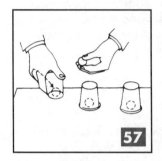

58 In a smooth, unbroken motion with your right hand, turn the cup mouth down and place it on the table in its former position. If the action of setting the cup down is done properly, the ball will remain hidden in the cup as the mouth of the cup comes to rest on the table.

59 At this point, you have apparently lifted the right-hand cup, picked up the ball that was under it, and replaced the cup on the table. Really, you have secretly loaded the fourth ball into the cup.

60 Once the cup is on the table, openly transfer the ball from your left hand to your right hand.

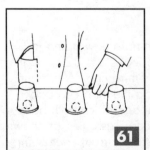

61 Place your right hand in your pocket, apparently leaving the ball there. Actually, you secretly retain the ball in the finger-palm position and remove your right hand from your pocket with the ball concealed in your right fingers.

NOTE: Steps 55 through 61 are the key moves in Phase 4. The spectators will be convinced that the first cup is empty and that the ball is now in your pocket.

62 Repeat this same sequence of moves (Steps 55 through 61) with the center cup, secretly loading the extra ball into the cup as you apparently place the visible ball in your pocket.

63 Once again, repeat the sequence (Steps 55 through 61) with the last cup, up to the point where your hand is in your pocket, apparently leaving the ball there.

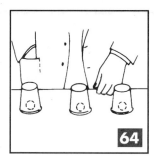

64 The situation at this point should look as shown in the illustration. Unknown to the spectators, there is one ball under each cup, and the extra ball is in your pocket with the three lemons. The spectators think you have placed all three balls, one at a time, in your right pocket. Really, you have secretly loaded the balls back under the three cups. You could stop now by merely revealing the "return" of the three balls. However, don't make that revelation quite yet. Continue to Phase 5.

NOTE: The next series of moves is based on the same secret loading process that you have just learned. Practice the moves thoroughly, until you can load each cup quickly and smoothly without undue attention to your right hand.

PHASE 5 — LEMON SURPRISE

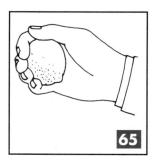

65 When your right hand is in your pocket in Step 64, release the ball and grasp one of the three lemons, curling your fingers around it as far as possible. Remove your hand from your pocket, secretly holding the lemon, and let your hand fall casually to your side. Be sure to use a lemon (or potato or small rubber ball) that can be totally concealed from view as you hold it in your hand, as shown.

66 As your right hand secretly holds the lemon, grasp the cup on the right with your left hand in readiness to lift it from the table. Then, as you lift the cup to reveal the ball beneath it, bring your right hand up from your side, making sure to keep the back of your hand to the spectators.
The surprise appearance of the ball under this cup will draw the eyes of the spectators to the table.

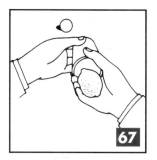

67 In the same motion, turn the cup mouth upward with your left hand and place it in your right hand, as shown here from your viewpoint. Be sure the fingers and the back of your right hand completely cover the top of the cup, so that the spectators cannot see between your hand and the mouth of the cup.

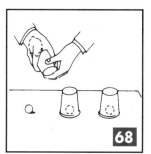

68 This illustration shows the action from the spectators' point of view. It is very important that you practice these critical moves in front of a mirror in order to observe the spectators' view of the presentation, as well as your own.

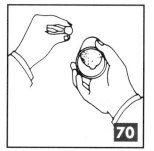

69 As soon as you transfer the cup to your right hand, move your left hand to the table and pick up the now visible ball. At the same time, allow the lemon to drop unseen into the cup.

70 From your point of view, this loading action looks like this. Be sure to keep the mouth of the cup tilted toward you during this procedure.

71 As you lift the ball from the table with your left hand, swing the cup mouth down and place it on the table with your right hand, as shown. The important point here is to execute this movement smoothly and quickly, keeping the lemon well within the cup and out of sight of the spectators.

72 Openly transfer the ball from your left hand to your right hand and place it in your right pocket. While your hand is in the pocket, grasp another lemon in readiness to load the next cup.

73 Repeat the exact same sequence (Steps 65 through 72) with the center cup. Just go back to Step 65 and repeat all of the steps through Step 72 with the second cup, ending with a lemon secretly loaded under the cup and your right hand in your pocket, grasping the third lemon.

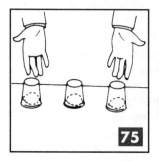

74 Repeat Steps 65 through 72 with the third cup, ending with a lemon secretly loaded under it as well.

75 When the last ball is placed in your pocket, leave it there and remove your empty right hand. The three cups now each conceal a lemon beneath them. The spectators believe that you merely placed the three balls back into your pocket and that the cups are now empty.

76 To bring the routine to its startling and spectacular conclusion, ask a spectator if there is a ball under any of the cups. No matter what the answer is, lift the cup the spectator points to, revealing the lemon beneath it! The appearance of the first lemon will catch your spectators completely off guard.

77 Without hesitation, quickly lift the other two cups, one at a time, revealing the other two lemons.

COMMENTS AND SUGGESTIONS

CUPS AND BALLS is probably the oldest and certainly one of the most popular tricks in magic. The necessary props (three cups and four balls) may be purchased at any good magic supply company. For practice purposes, and even for your first performances, a practical set of "cups" may be made from paper cups. The heavy paper kind is best (the type used for coffee or other hot beverages). These cups are strong and usually have a slightly recessed bottom. The cups can be decorated by painting them an attractive color, if you wish.

A professional set of balls may be made of cork or hard rubber. Sometimes a cork ball with a knitted or crocheted cover is used. You may also make your first set of balls as well. Balls made from sponge rubber are excellent for practice. They are quite easy to make and equally easy to handle during the presentation.

Though the basic moves are relatively simple, they should be practiced until they become almost automatic, in order to perform a convincing routine. Any hesitation on your part may detract from the effect, as the whole purpose is to keep just enough ahead of the spectators so that they are constantly wondering what will happen next. In placing the balls beneath the cups, or pretending to do so, the moves must be natural and identical to one another. Once your actions become automatic, the vital moves will begin to feel more casual and less conspicuous, and therefore less likely to arouse suspicion. Another reason for continued practice is that of gaining self-confidence. When first performing the CUPS AND BALLS, you may wonder just why the routine deceives people. This is particularly true when you load the lemons at the finish. Having watched the small balls jump from cup to cup, spectators become so caught up with the action of the balls on the table that they are never ready for the unexpected appearance of the lemons.

CUPS AND BALLS is especially suited for performing while seated at a table, but it can be worked just as well when standing at a table. Any points of individuality that you may add to the routine will most likely prove helpful. Some performers like to vary it by using either hand to turn over a cup, even though the hand may have a ball palmed at the time. Just think of CUPS AND BALLS as your trick, to be done the way you like it most. Once you have mastered CUPS AND BALLS, you will be able to present one of the finest and most respected effects in the   Art of Magic.

CHAPTER 5

SPONGE SORCERY TRICKS

SPONGE SORCERY, performed with sponge balls or sponge cubes, is a distinctive type of magic. Originally, magic tricks evolved around common objects such as cards, coins, and matches because they were "natural" objects to carry or borrow for magical purposes.

Then magicians began carving sponge balls out of rubber sponges. Magicians found that because sponge balls were compressible, they could be handled with ease and secrecy. As different weights, textures, and compressibility of synthetic sponges emerged, sponge sorcery became increasingly popular. Today sponge balls have a fairly solid look, causing spectators to overlook their compressibility. Sponge balls are also easier to manipulate than their predecessors.

Sponge cubes are also popular with many performers. They are cubical in shape and are handled the same as sponge balls. But because sponge sorcery routines are usually performed at a table, sponge cubes have the advantage of never rolling off. Thus they are easier to use in a close-up setting. You can easily make sponge cubes by cutting soft foam rubber into 1" cubes. You may also make sponge balls from soft sponge or buy them from a magic supply store.

Whichever type you choose, you'll find the following routine well worth the effort required to learn it. Once you have seen the delighted response of your audience, chances are SPONGE SORCERY will become a permanent part of your close-up magic act.

SPONGE SORCERY

EFFECT

The performer magically causes three sponges to appear, multiply, and vanish in an entertaining and amusing manner. They even seem to multiply in the hands of a spectator!

SECRET AND PREPARATION

Before the performance, place three sponges in your right pants pocket and one sponge in your left pants pocket.

METHOD

Sponge balls are used in the following illustrations. To practice and present your routine, you may substitute sponge cubes in place of the balls, as shown.

A SPONGE APPEARS

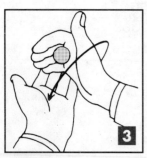

1 With the four sponges located in your pants pockets, as described, casually place your hand in your right pants pocket. Grasp one of the sponges in the finger-palm position (see FINGER-PALM VANISH page 70) and remove your hand, holding the sponge secretly. Reach into the air and produce it at the tips of your right fingers. You can also produce the sponge from the spectator's coat lapel, from behind the spectator's ear, or any other appropriate place.

2 As you display the first sponge in your right hand, position it in readiness for the FINGER-PALM VANISH, by placing it on your open hand at the base of the second and third fingers, as shown. The left hand lies casually, palm down, on the table.

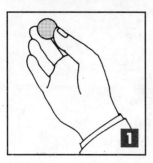

3 In one smooth, flowing movement, bring both hands together, turning them over as you do. This is done on the pretense of gently tossing the sponge from your right hand into your left hand. But instead of actually tossing the sponge into the left hand, it is secretly retained in the second and third fingers of the right hand, in the finger-palm position.

4 Move your right hand away (with the sponge), as you close your left hand into a loose fist. The first finger of your right hand should casually point toward your left fist, as shown in the illustration.

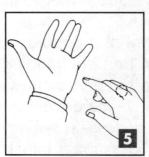

5 Pause for a moment and then make a crumpling motion with your left fingers as if to cause the sponge to "dissolve" in your hand. Open your left hand to show that the sponge has vanished.

NOTE: What you have just done is the basic FINGER-PALM VANISH with a sponge. Practice it with the sponge until it becomes smooth and convincing. When done correctly, the spectators should not suspect that you really retain the sponge in your right hand.

FLIGHT TO THE POCKET

7 Explain to the spectators that often, when a sponge vanishes, it manages to reappear in your right pocket. Reach into your right pants pocket (being careful not to flash the vanished sponge that is now concealed in your right fingers) and grasp one of the two sponges that are left in that pocket.

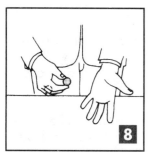

8 Openly remove this sponge from your pocket, keeping the first sponge finger-palmed. Display it in your right fingertips. Again, be careful not to let the spectators see the sponge finger-palmed in your right hand, as you display the other sponge. The effect is that you vanished a sponge from your left hand and

caused it to reappear in your pants pocket.

GUESS WHICH HAND

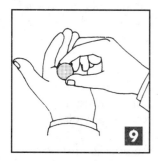

9 Upon completing the "Flight to the Pocket," you now hold one sponge at your right fingertips and one sponge secretly in the finger-palm position of the same hand. Openly place the sponge from your right fingertips into the palm of your left hand, as shown.

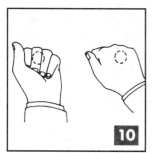

10 Close your left hand into a fist and hold it palm up in front of you, as shown. Close your right hand and hold it palm down next to your left fist. The spectators still believe that only one sponge is being used and that it is in your left hand.

11 Strike both fists together several times and hold your hands crossed at the wrist, as shown. Explain how this seems to have a strange effect on the location of the mischievous sponge. With that, ask the spectator which hand the sponge is in.

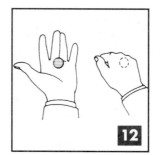

12 The answer will probably be, "In your left hand." No matter which hand the spectator says, uncross your hands and open your left hand, revealing that the sponge is still there.

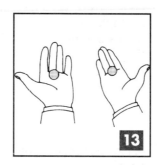

13 State that it really didn't matter which hand was chosen; the spectator would have been correct in either case. With that, turn your right hand palm up and open the fingers, revealing the other sponge. It appears that the strange effect you spoke about has caused one sponge to multiply into two.

SPECTATOR'S DOUBLES

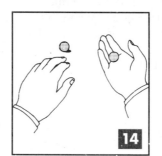

14 Place the left-hand sponge on the table and hold the right-hand sponge in position for the FINGER-PALM VANISH.

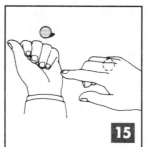

15 Pretend to place the sponge in your left hand. Actually you execute the FINGER-PALM VANISH, secretly retaining the sponge in your right hand. Remember that each time you perform this vanish, your left hand should be closed in a loose fist as if it actually contained the sponge.

16 Without hesitation, move your right hand toward the sponge lying on the table. Be careful not to expose the sponge finger-palmed in your right hand.

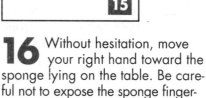

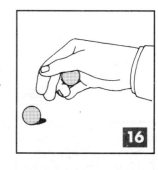

17 As your right hand arrives above the sponge on the table, secretly place the finger-palmed sponge directly on top of the sponge on the table.

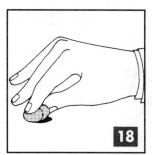

18 By drawing your right hand along the table, the sponges will roll toward the tips of your right fingers, where they can be picked up together as one sponge. Because of the soft texture of the sponges when they are pinched together slightly, this will appear to be just one sponge.

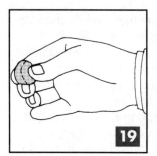

19 As you display the two sponges as one at the tips of your right fingers, ask the spectator to open their right hand and hold it palm up above the table.

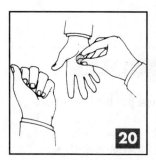

20 Place the sponge(s) in the spectator's hand as you state, "Here, you hold this sponge in your hand while I hold the other." At this point, everyone thinks that you still hold one sponge in your left hand and that you are merely giving the spectator the other sponge to hold, when actually you are giving the spectator both sponges.

21 Instruct the spectator to close their fingers around the sponge and to squeeze it tightly so it would be impossible for you to remove it without their knowledge. Be sure you maintain a firm grip on the two sponges until the spectator's fingers are completely closed around them. Then, and only then, should you remove your fingers from the fist.

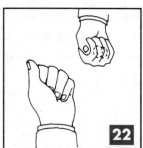

22 Explain that you intend to cause the sponge that you are holding to travel invisibly from your hand into the spectator's closed fist.

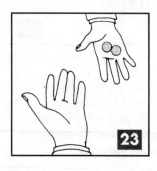

23 Again, make a crumpling motion with your left fingers and open your hand to show it is empty. Ask the spectator if anything happened. Whatever the answer, tell the spectator to open their hand, revealing the two sponges.

TRANSPOSITION IN YOUR HANDS

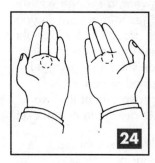

24 Take both sponges from the spectator and place them on the table in front of you about 12" apart. Turn your hands palm up and openly place the back of your hands on top of the sponges, as shown. This is the starting position for the next series of moves.

NOTE: Steps 25 through 36 are a clever sequence of moves designed to confuse and amaze the spectators.

25 Raise your right hand, turn it over, and pick up the sponge that was beneath it with the tips of your right thumb and finger.

26 Without lifting your left hand from the table, rest the sponge in the palm of your left hand. Close your hand into a fist over your right fingers and the sponge. As you do this say, "The right sponge goes in your left hand." Withdraw your right fingers, actually leaving the sponge in your closed left hand.

27 Raise your left fist off the table and pick up the sponge that was beneath it with the tips of the right fingers. Close your right fingers into a fist around the sponge. Hold your right fist next to your left fist as you say, "And the left sponge goes into the right hand."

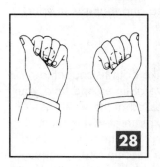

28 You now hold one sponge in each hand, as shown in the illustration.

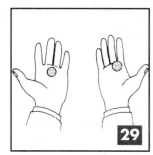

29 Open both hands together revealing the two sponges, one in each hand. So far, no magic has happened! State that you will now do the same thing again. Unknown to the spectators, this trial run is a very important part of the mystery that is about to take place. By first executing this series of moves without any magic, you condition the spectators to expect the same results next time.

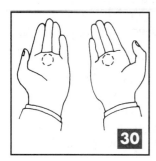

30 Again, place both hands on top of the two sponges in the starting position for the same series of moves.

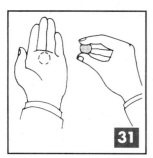

31 Again, raise your right hand, turn it over, and pick up the sponge beneath it in the tips of the right fingers (just as you did in Step 25).

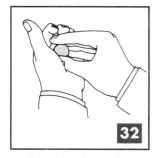

32 Rest the sponge in the palm of the left hand and close your left fingers over your right fingers and the sponge. Again you say, "The right sponge goes in the left fist." This time, however, instead of leaving the sponge in your left fist, as you withdraw your right hand, secretly retain the sponge between your right thumb and fingers. Be sure to keep your right fingers together so that the spectators cannot see the sponge between them.

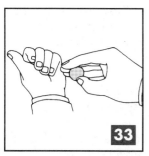

33 Immediately move your right hand away from your closed left hand, secretly carrying the sponge in your right hand, as shown. Direct your complete attention toward your left hand, as if it really contained the sponge. As your right hand moves away, draw your right thumb inward, moving the sponge slightly deeper into your hand, where it will not be seen by the spectators.

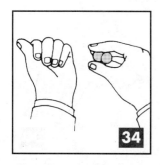

34 Raise your left hand and, with your right fingers, pick up the sponge that lay beneath it. When you pick up the left-hand sponge, secretly add the palmed right-hand sponge to it (just as you did in Step 18).

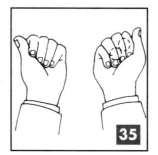

35 Close your right hand into a fist around the two sponges. Hold your right fist next to your left fist, as shown. To the spectators, you have apparently just repeated Steps 24 through 28, and they think that you now hold one sponge in each hand.

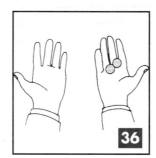

36 Make a crumpling motion with your left fingers and open your left hand to show that the sponge has vanished. Slowly open your right hand, revealing both sponges! It appears as though one sponge has jumped invisibly from your left hand into your right hand!

IMPOSSIBLE PENETRATION

NOTE: If you have been sitting at a table as you perform the trick, you must now stand up for the next portion of the routine. Steps 37 through 44 are shown from the spectators' viewpoint. (You should have an extra sponge in your left pocket before beginning Step 37.)

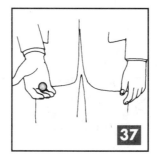

37 After "Transposition in Your Hands," place one sponge on the table and keep the other sponge in your right hand, in position for the FINGER-PALM VANISH.

38 Execute the FINGER-PALM VANISH, pretending to place the sponge in your left hand, but actually retaining it finger-palmed in your right hand.

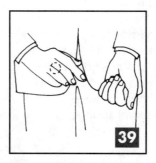

39 Hold your closed left hand in a loose fist, as if it actually contained the sponge, and casually move your right hand (with the finger-palmed sponge) away. Again be sure to direct your complete attention toward your left fist.

40 Place your left hand (which supposedly contains the sponge) into your left pants pocket, as you explain that your clothes are made of a special material.

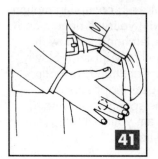

41 With that, move your right hand (which secretly holds the other sponge) in front of your left pants pocket. Your left hand is still inside your pocket. With your right hand, press the sponge against your pants leg next to where your left hand is inside your pocket.

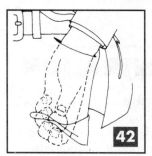

42 Inside your pocket, your left thumb and fingers grasp the sponge through the fabric and hold it between the folds of the cloth so that it is concealed from view by the material. As soon as the sponge is in position, move your right hand away from in front of your pant leg. The pinched section of the fabric will look like a fold in the cloth.

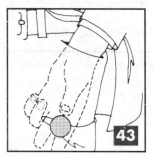

43 Immediately begin a back-and-forth rubbing motion with your left fingers. At the same time, relax your grip on the sponge through the fabric. This will cause the sponge to slowly emerge into view as though it were penetrating right through the cloth.

NOTE: This illusion is very effective. Don't worry if the sponge is not completely hidden in the folds of the fabric before you remove your right hand. It will just appear that the penetration of the cloth started when you first placed your right hand on your pants leg.

44 When the sponge emerges almost totally into view, grasp it in your right hand and pull it away from the pocket. At the same time, with your left hand, secretly secure the sponge already in that pocket in the finger-palm position. While all the attention is on the sponge in your right hand, remove your left hand from your pocket with the new secret sponge.

SPECTATOR'S HAND REVISITED

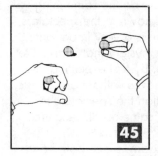

45 There are now three sponges in play, although the spectators are aware of only two. One sponge is on the table, another is held at the tips of your right fingers, and the secret sponge is finger-palmed in your left hand.

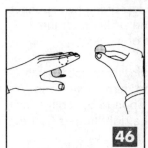

46 Call attention to the sponge in your right hand. While the spectators are looking at it, with your left hand, pick up the sponge on the table and add the secret sponge to it.

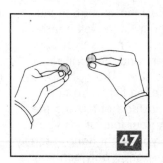

47 With your left hand, display the sponge that was on the table and the secret sponge as one, holding them with your left thumb and fingers. At this point you actually hold three sponges (one in your right hand and two in your left). To the spectators, it appears that you hold only one sponge in each hand.

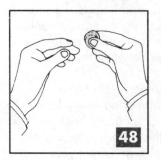

48 Transfer the two sponges in your left hand to your right hand, placing them directly on top of the sponge in your right fingers. Say, "Now I would like you to hold these two sponges."

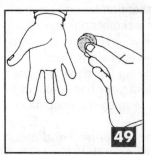

49 Move your right hand (which now holds the three sponges) toward the spectator and ask the spectator to open their hand to take the sponges from you.

50 Place all three sponges in the spectator's hand. Instruct the spectator to close the fingers around them. Tell the spectator to squeeze their fist tightly to make sure that you cannot remove them. Again, remember to wait until the spectator's hand is completely closed before releasing your grip on the sponges.

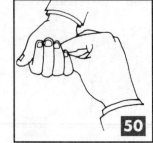

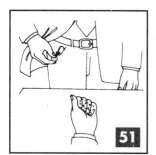

51 Once the spectator has a firm grip on the sponges, reach into your right pants pocket and remove the fourth sponge from your pocket. Openly display the sponge as you say, "You may be wondering how all this is happening. Well, the secret is that I have a third sponge that nobody knows about."

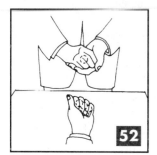

52 With that, execute the FINGER-PALM VANISH, pretending to place the sponge into your left hand, but actually retaining it in the finger-palm position in your right hand.

53 Casually drop your right hand to the table and move your closed left fist next to the spectator's hand.

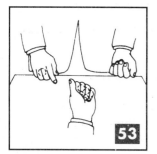

54 Make the crumpling motion with your left fingers and open your hand to show it empty. Instruct the spectator to open their hand, revealing all three sponges. It appears that the third sponge has flown invisibly from your fingers into the spectator's hand.

TWO IN THE HAND, ONE IN THE POCKET—PART ONE

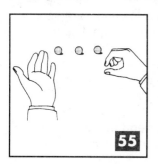

55 After the "Spectator's Hand Revisited," there are four sponges in use, although the spectators are only aware of three. The next sequence begins with the three sponges in a horizontal row in front of you and the fourth sponge held secretly in your curled right fingers.

56 With your right hand, pick up the sponge at the right end of the row, and execute the "two-as-one" pickup, as in Steps 17 and 18. In your right hand, you now hold two sponges together as one.

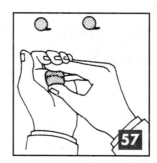

57 Place the two sponges in the palm of your left hand and close your left fingers around them as you say, "One in the hand."

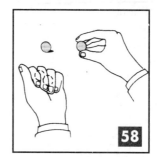

58 Withdraw your right hand from your left fist. Pick up another of the sponges on the table with your right hand, as shown.

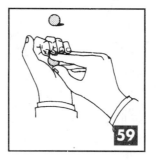

59 Move your right hand toward your left fist. Open your left fingers just enough to place the sponge in your left hand. Say, "Two in the hand." Close your left fingers around the three sponges and withdraw your right hand from your left fist.

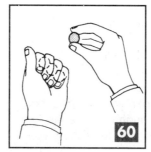

60 Pick up the remaining sponge in your right hand.

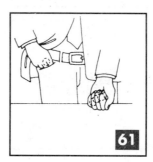

61 Openly place the last sponge in your right pants pocket. Say, "And one in the pocket." As your hand reaches in your right pants pocket, do not leave the sponge in your pocket. Instead, hold it in the finger-palm position and remove your hand from your pocket, secretly carrying the sponge along. The spectators will believe that you merely placed the sponge in your pocket.

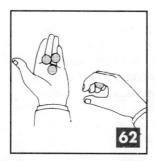

62 Ask the spectator, "How many sponges are in my hand?" The answer will be, "Two." Open your left hand, revealing three sponges, as you remark, "Maybe I went too fast. I'll do that again."

TWO IN THE HAND, ONE IN THE POCKET—PART TWO

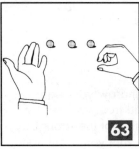

63 With your left hand, place the three sponges in a horizontal row on the table as in Step 55. The fourth sponge is secretly held in the curled fingers of your right hand.

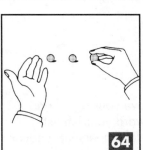

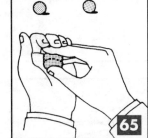

64 As before, execute the "two-as-one" pickup with the sponge on the right, as in Step 56.

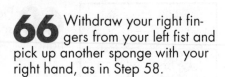

65 Place the two sponges as one in your left hand and close your left fingers into a fist around them, as in Step 57. Say, "One in the hand."

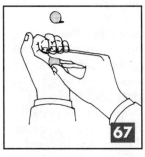

66 Withdraw your right fingers from your left fist and pick up another sponge with your right hand, as in Step 58.

67 Open your left fingers just enough to place the sponge into your left fist, as you did in Step 59. Say, "Two in the hand."

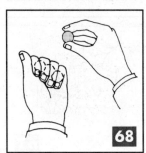

68 Pick up the remaining sponge in your right fingertips, as in Step 60.

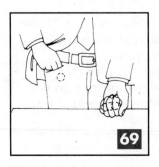

69 Say, "And one in the pocket." Openly place this sponge into your right pants pocket, the same as in Step 61, but this time, leave the sponge in your pocket.

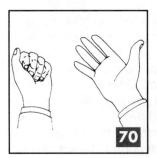

70 Withdraw your right hand from your pocket and gesture toward your fist. Make the gesture in such a way that the spectators can see that your right hand is quite empty. Do not call special attention to your right hand, merely show it in an open and casual manner, so that there is no question that it is empty.

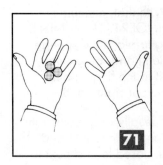

71 As you gesture ask, "How many in the hand?" The answer will probably be "Two." The spectators are so baffled by this time, however, that there is no predicting what they will say! In any event, open your left hand revealing all three sponges. Now say, "Let's try just once more."

TOTAL VANISH

Now for a smashing climax to the routine!

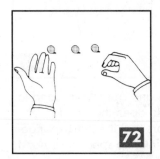

72 At this time, there are only three sponges remaining. With your left hand, place them on the table in a row, as you did before.

73 Begin again, just as you did before, by picking up the sponge on the far right with your right thumb and fingers. Rest this sponge on the palm of your open left hand.

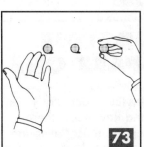

74 Close the fingers of your left hand around the sponge and the fingers of your right hand. Your right fingers retain their grip on the sponge. Say, "One in the hand." Your right fingers continue to hold the sponge in your closed left hand.

75 Instead of leaving the sponge in your left hand, secretly retain the sponge in your right fingers, as you withdraw your right hand from your left fist.

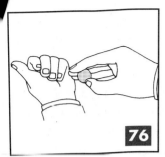

76 To keep the sponge concealed from view during this procedure, as you withdraw your hand move your right thumb slightly inward, rolling the sponge behind your right fingers out of sight.

77 Without hesitation, move your right hand toward the next sponge and execute the "two-as-one" pickup, as in Step 17.

78 With the two sponges held together, as one, in your right hand, open your left fist just enough to place your right fingers into your hand. Say, "Two in the hand."

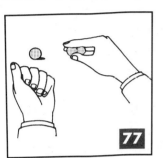

Once again, your thumb secretly draws both sponges out of view behind your right fingers.

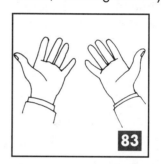

79 At the same time, you withdraw your right fingers from your left hand and close your left hand into a loose fist.

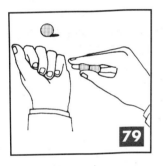

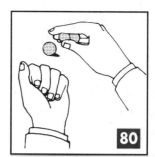

80 Without pausing, pick up the remaining sponge in your right hand. Do not execute the "two-as-one" pickup. Just keep the two palmed sponges behind your fingers and openly pick up the third sponge, holding it at the fingertips of your right hand.

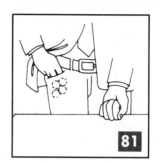

81 Immediately, place your right hand into your right pants pocket. Say, "And the last sponge goes in the pocket." Leave all three sponges in your pocket.

82 Remove your right hand from your pocket. With your right hand, gesture toward your left fist so that the spectators can see that your right hand is quite empty.

83 Ask, "How many in my hand?" By now, the spectators will probably answer, "Three," thinking that they know what is going to happen. Whatever number is given, say, "No, actually they are all gone, because that was the end of the trick." With that, open your left hand to show that all three sponges have vanished, bringing the routine to a startling climax!

COMMENTS AND SUGGESTIONS

It is generally good policy to avoid handling sponges either too boldly or too cautiously. A quick thrust of the hand excites suspicion, and so does a tight squeeze of the sponge itself when the performer is actually giving the spectator two as one. A casual in-between course is best, particularly when done in an unhurried manner. In fact, the correct preliminary procedure will do much toward dispelling suspicion on the part of the spectators.

If a sponge is held lightly at the fingertips, with absolutely no pressure, no one is apt to regard it as compressible; and, later, when two are shown as one, correct pressure of the thumb and fingers can give the double ball a distinctively single appearance. While a natural, unhurried motion of the hand is sufficient to cover the deception, larger loads depend upon fuller compression for complete concealment.

When practicing, it is a good idea to break the routine down into smaller units. Learn each phase before you go on to the next. SPONGE SORCERY is undoubtedly one of the finest close-up tricks in magic. Each effect in this routine can be performed separately; and as you will see when you perform it for your friends, the entire routine is constructed in a logical progression, building to a perfect climax—truly a masterpiece of magic!

GLOSSARY

ACCORDION PLEAT: Method of folding a handkerchief or paper, in much the same manner as the bellows of an accordion are designed to expand and contract.

BOW KNOT: Specialty rope-tie with magical applications, similar to the type of knot used when tying one's shoes.

CLOSE-UP MAGIC: Magic tricks that can be performed at close quarters to an audience. Card and coin tricks, among others, are generally referred to as close-up tricks.

CORING: Procedure of removing the center strands found in some types of cotton rope to make the rope more pliable and easy to work with.

CUP-AND-BALL TRICK: A true classic magic trick in which three balls mysteriously vanish and change places when covered by three inverted cups.

CUT-AND-RESTORED EFFECT: Any effect in which an object, usually a rope or handkerchief, is cut into one or more pieces, then magically returned to normal.

DO-AS-I-DO EFFECT: Any trick in which a spectator is asked to follow the actions of the magician.

DOUBLE-WALLED BAG: A paper bag used to vanish or change objects, thanks to a secret compartment made by gluing part of a second bag inside the first.

EFFECT: Description of how a magic trick looks to an audience.

FINGER-PALM POSITION: One of the many methods of concealing a coin or other small object by holding it with the fingers and keeping the hand in a natural position.

FORCED PAPERS/SLIPS: Slips of paper that the magician makes an audience member take, although the spectator thinks it is a free choice.

FORCING: A method in which a spectator thinks they have a free choice of a card or other object, when in fact, the magician knows ahead of time which one will be selected.

MAGIC CIRCLE: Term used to describe the imaginary powers of any circle written on a piece of paper and used in a magic performance.

METHOD: Description of how a magic trick works.

PADDLE MOVE: A type of manipulation used to apparently show both sides of a two-sided object, yet the audience actually sees the same side at all times. This is accomplished by well-practiced wrist and finger movements.

PENETRATION: One of the many subcategories of magic tricks, specifically, the apparent ability to pass one solid object through another.

PRESTIDIGITATOR: Another term for "magician." Its most literal translation, from French, means "fast fingers."

ROPE COILING: Loosely wrapping rope into a bundle.

SILKS: Term used to describe colorful silk handkerchiefs used by professional magicians.

SPECTRUM PREDICTION: One of many effective mental sorcery tricks, in which the magician pretends to read the minds of the audience.

SPONGE SORCERY: General term used to describe tricks and routines performed with sponge rubber balls.

THREADING THE NEEDLE: Rope trick in which one end of a piece of rope is apparently threaded through a small loop, faster than the eye can follow.

TRANSPOSITION: The apparent, invisible transfer of an object from one place to another.